The Anatomy of
PROPHECY

Books by Daniel Logan

THE RELUCTANT PROPHET
DO YOU HAVE ESP?
YOUR EASTERN STAR
AMERICA BEWITCHED
THE ANATOMY OF PROPHECY

The Anatomy of
PROPHECY

By Daniel Logan

PRENTICE-HALL, INC.
Englewood Cliffs, New Jersey

The Anatomy of Prophecy
by Daniel Logan
Copyright © 1975 by Daniel Logan
All rights reserved. No part of this book may be
reproduced in any form or by any means, except
for the inclusion of brief quotations in a review,
without permission in writing from the publisher.
Printed in the United States of America
Prentice-Hall International, Inc., London
Prentice-Hall of Australia, Pty. Ltd., Sydney
Prentice-Hall of Canada, Ltd., Toronto
Prentice-Hall of India Private Ltd., New Delhi
Prentice-Hall of Japan, Inc., Tokyo

10 9 8 7 6 5 4 3 2 1

Library of Congress Cataloging in Publication Data

Logan, Daniel
  The anatomy of prophecy.

  Bibliography: p.
  Includes index.
  1. Prophecies (Occult sciences)   I. Title.
BF1791.L63   133.3'2   74–23151
ISBN 0–13–035188–1

For Yuki
(June 5, 1970—May 9, 1974)

❧

My friend, my protector, my karma—
May flights of angels sing thee to thy rest.

Introduction

When one chooses to use the word "prophecy" in regard to psychic ability, the door is open to various lines of attack and criticism. I have heard from more than one person that they did not read my autobiography, *The Reluctant Prophet,* because it was "most presumptuous of you to utilize the sacred word of 'prophet' in referring to yourself." In actuality, it was a word chosen in innocence, mostly because it sounded more aesthetic than synonyms such as "psychic," "clairvoyant," and the like.

There are several definitions of the word "prophet" in the dictionary. In relation to my own ability in the area of prophecy, I use the definition of a prophet as "one who predicts or foretells what is to come by various means of interpretation." I shy away from the definition that states a prophet is "one who speaks for God or some Deity by divine inspiration."

I believe that much of the confusion that arises in utilizing the term "prophecy" stems from its usage in the Bible, where many of the characters are referred to as prophets—almost all of them for different reasons. Abraham was tabbed a prophet because he is, quite literally, stated as being the friend of God. Aaron and his brother Moses (as well as their sister Miriam) are also called prophets—Moses because he was the appointed speaker of divine laws, Aaron since he was the translator of the divine laws into daily practice. Miriam is called a prophetess because she was the leader in songs and dances that praised God. Each of them had some special relationship with Yahweh (God), but throughout the Bible, persons with special gifts or abilities are also called prophets.

vii

I do not equate my prophetic ability with that of the prophets in the Bible; on the other hand, I am well aware that any prophetic ability is a gift from a higher source. So is any other ability, be it the creation of a work of art or the accomplishment of certain labors which help to assist, enlighten, or in some way bring about physical, mental, or spiritual well-being to one's fellow man.

What is important is what one chooses to *do* with a gift. I have often said that I believe the only real sin in the world is a person's choosing *not* to use a given ability, no matter how small the gift may appear. The misuse of an ability is a part of the original sin.

I see abilities, or gifts or talents, as karmic in nature. That which we have done before, we are given the opportunity to do again. In each succeeding life the ability should be strengthened, utilized to its utmost, and directly tied into one's karmic pattern—past, present, and future. The soul cannot progress if abilities are hidden and not used in any given lifetime.

In a well-known Noel Coward song there is a line that says: "I merely have the talent to amuse." This is by no means a meager ability. For if in amusing someone, one makes that person's burden easier, even for a brief moment, then the one who is "amusing" has utilized his gift in the correct way.

I have become progressively aware that in my own past lives I did not utilize my prophetic abilities in the most positive manner. In some instances I chose not to use the talent at all. Let us say that in this life, I am trying.

Daniel Logan
New York

Contents

"The most distressing thing that can happen to a prophet is to be proved wrong; the next most distressing thing is to be proved right."

—Aldous Huxley

"Before the sun rose he was harnassed light,
And to the field goes he; where every flower
Did, as a prophet,
Weep what it foresaw. . . ."

—William Shakespeare
TROILUS AND CRESSIDA

The Anatomy of
PROPHECY

ONE

The Foreseeable Future

"Don't go out next week," I blurted out. "I mean, don't get into a yellow car. If you do, something negative will happen and you could be harmed in some way."

The lady, who had come to me for a psychic consultation in my New York City office, sat upright in her chair.

She turned slightly pale. The prediction, quite naturally, had upset her. She paused for a moment and then asked if I had any other feelings that related to the predicted occurrence.

"No," I said. "That's all I get on it." The consultation continued, then came to an end, and the lady left.

As is the case with many of my psychic readings, I did not expect to hear from her again. But exactly ten days later she telephoned me.

"Well, thank God you were wrong, Mr. Logan. I was not involved in an accident."

1

"I'm most happy to hear that," I told her. "I'd much rather be wrong in such an instance."

"You see," she continued, "you frightened me so very much that I didn't get into *any* vehicle all last week. I made sure that your prediction couldn't happen. I use taxicabs quite often in my work, usually yellow cabs in Manhattan, but I walked to and from my office."

She continued to tell me how glad she was that I had been wrong, but I could tell by her manner that she was a bit put out that the accident hadn't occurred! The question of "What *can* I believe that he told me?" was quite apparent in her tone.

After she mentioned the non-accident several more times, I began to become annoyed that she just didn't leave it alone and be happy my prediction hadn't come to pass.

"If you had gotten into a cab or another yellow car, how do you know that you wouldn't have been involved in some kind of mishap?" I finally asked.

Then, after a moment of silence on the other end of the phone: "Well, I guess we'll never know that, will we?"

Her voice had taken on a decidedly superior tone and my Taurean temper had to be held in check. I had a fleeting regret at having told her the prediction, but I realized that was the wrong attitude on my part.

I forgot all about the lady until six or seven months later, when I gave a lecture at Town Hall in New York City. After the lecture, several people gathered around asking questions about themselves and future world conditions. The woman who hadn't been involved in a yellow car mishap was one of the crowd. She waited until I was relatively alone and then approached me.

"Mr. Logan," she said nervously, "I just wanted you to know that something very odd occurred in regard to your prediction. You remember, the one about the yellow car?"

I nodded politely.

"I don't know if this means anything, but my son has a light yellow car; and on the Sunday of the week that you gave me the warning, he and my daughter-in-law had a terrific argument. It started at breakfast and continued in their car on the way to church. It ended up in her leaving him and instigating divorce proceedings. They hadn't been getting along for months, but had kept their troubles from me."

I could see that she was fighting back tears and was finding it difficult to relate the story. She composed herself and continued: "What they were arguing about was an abortion which my daughter-in-law wanted to have. She doesn't want a third child. The argument was so violent that it was becoming physical, and my son finally had to pull over to the curb." She sighed deeply. "What I am trying to say is that—well, I was supposed to have visited their home that weekend. I most certainly would have attended church services with them as I usually do, and I am so completely against abortion that I most certainly would have gotten involved." Her mouth twitched. "Mr. Logan, my question to you is, could this have been the warning you gave me? You simply said that I should not get into a yellow car that week, because something negative would happen and that I might be harmed. You didn't say that anything *physical* would happen to me, but that's what I then thought you meant."

I told her that I honestly couldn't say that this was what my warning had been. But on the other hand, neither could I truthfully state that this *wasn't* the meaning of the prediction.

"Anyway," she continued, "I am so glad I wasn't in that car, and I'm grateful for the warning you gave me. I'm sure you prevented me from becoming involved in their argument. I apologize for the phone call I made to you. I do realize that your psychic work enables you to help people avoid making mistakes by seeing the possibilities, the outcome of a situation, without seeing or even understanding the situation itself."

I thanked her for telling me, and that evening, as I was meditating before going to sleep, I thought of her words—that I could see the possibilities and not necessarily the situation itself. I have given psychic readings and made prophecies that seemingly meant nothing until years later, when the subject was able to interpret and apply the prophecy to his own life. And the lady's story reminded me of something that had just broken via the news media involving a world prophecy I had made.

At the end of each year I usually make predictions for the upcoming year involving world events and international personalities. This particular year was 1967, the year before the presidential elections. I was giving my predictions over NBC radio as guest on the long-running nationally syndicated Long John Nebel Show.

While Mr. Nebel and I were discussing the elections from a psychic standpoint, I predicted that the candidates would most probably be either George Romney or Richard Nixon on the Republican ticket, and Hubert Humphrey (Lyndon Johnson had already declared that he would not run again) on the Democratic ticket.

"Wait a minute, Dan," Mr. Nebel said in his irascible, direct manner, "what about Bob Kennedy? He's the most likely candidate on the Democratic ticket. In fact, he's the Democrat's only chance."

At that time, the talk was centered around there being no question that Robert Kennedy would be the candidate the Democrats would choose to place in the running.

"Well?" Mr. Nebel demanded.

"There will never be another Kennedy in the White House," I finally stated.

Everyone involved in the media has heard of Jeanne Dixon's prediction about the assassination of President

John Kennedy, and they usually take heed when any psychic makes a prediction concerning the Kennedys, especially a negative one. But Long John Nebel did not let the subject lie there.

"Why, Dan? Can you tell us why there will not be another Kennedy in the White House?"

I said that I would rather not talk about it, but that psychically I felt if Robert Kennedy or his brother Ted were to attempt to get into the White House, there would be more tragedies.

"Well, at least he'll be nominated, won't he?" Mr. Nebel asked.

"No," I replied, "he will not be the nominee."

I had received this psychic information one day while watching Robert Kennedy give a speech on television. My psychic impression was that he would not ever be the President, and that something would happen—not only to him, but to any Kennedy who might venture toward the office of President.

Psychic impressions regarding prophecies come to me in various ways. They can flash through my conscious mind while I am doing something entirely unrelated to psychic matters, such as hiking, reading a book, or even riding in a plane. Prophecies also come during meditation or when I am in an otherwise altered state of consciousness, such as a trance. (How this ability works when I am in altered states of awareness will be dealt with a bit later on.)

I have received many of my psychic impressions when watching television. My psychiatrist friends say that watching TV is a form of hypnotism, or a kind of heavy concentration and relaxation of the mind. This state affords the subconscious an opportunity to emerge and release information into the consciousness. The information may be actual events forgotten and stored in the subconscious over the years, or it may be pronounced psi occurrences. I have also found that the psychic vibrations around a person who is appearing on TV are quite easily picked up by the viewer.

After I had received the psychic impression that the Kennedy family would be involved in more tragedies if they sought the presidency, I went into a meditation and received the same psychic feeling. I could "see" an empty chair in front of the Presidential Seal.

Unfortunately, the prediction regarding the Kennedys did come to pass. The death of the young girl at Chappaquiddick prevented Ted Kennedy from emerging as a likely candidate in the 1972 elections. Every few years the words, "there will never be another Kennedy in the White House," spoken in 1967, come back to haunt me. And, something tragic will occur if he seeks the Presidency in 1976.

The karmic destiny of Rose Kennedy is most fascinating and very involved. In my meditations I have received psychic impressions that she is the one who may have attracted the family's negative karma. In previous lives, many persons, including those in her own family, were sacrificed so that she might advance in some power situation. I believe she was a man at that time. In this lifetime, Rose Kennedy had the choice to live out her life in a manner very different from the path she did choose. I feel that she has made many of the same karmic mistakes by not doing everything in her power to prevent her family from rising to top political offices and the high social position they have reached. None of the Kennedy story is coincidence. Years from now, when our country accepts the more spiritual aspects of life and fully understands the workings of reincarnation and karma, the Kennedy saga will be a most timely, fitting example.

Politically I would have voted for Robert Kennedy or any of the Kennedys, because I feel that the intentions of the Kennedy children were of a much higher level than those of their opponents. I did not particularly like Robert Kennedy, but felt him to be much more aligned with justice and truth than Richard Nixon.

The prophecies regarding the Kennedys and the one I gave to the lady about not getting into a yellow car were in the "probability" or conditional area of prophecy. Had the Kennedys not attempted to attain the presidency, I feel that the tragedies would not have occurred. These types of prophecies are typical of the kinds of predictions which need interpretation and which seem to depend on other factors.

Choice is a most important aspect of any psychic reading. I never say that a psychic impression I receive has a 100 percent chance of happening, nor do I believe that someone cannot change or alter a prediction once it is made. The future is preordained to a degree, but karmic choice must be seriously taken into account.

It is my belief that a psychic sees one side of a coin that is standing on end, about to fall. He may see which side has the stronger possibility of landing up after it falls, but he cannot be sure that the coin will not flip to the other side. The person to whom the prediction is being made does have a choice and should only be guided, rather than told that a certain event will happen no matter what. That is why I prefer to call my work in this field "psychic guidance" or "psychic advice."

Reincarnation must be taken into consideration too, and so I will not make choices or decisions for those who seek out my psychic advice. There was a time when I felt that I could not give psychic advice as it might tend to alter karmic destiny. It took many years before I was able to realize that in truth I was a part of my client's karmic destiny; that whoever might seek psychic guidance must have been placed on a path that would afford the information an opportunity to be passed on. What the person chooses to do with this advice is another matter altogether.

I refuse to become a "psychic crutch," this aspect of

my work can be, for some people, as addictive as alcohol or any other drug. I lived to regret the one period of my life when I allowed myself to be psychically used on almost a daily basis. The person who utilized my ability in this manner was soon not able to make any decisions on her own without first consulting me. A simple matter of daily routine, such as what store to shop at, became the basis of a hurried phone call or a meeting. There developed a most difficult situation, one that I would not ever allow myself to become involved in again.

It was during this trying time that I came to realize that there were certain situations in a person's life that could not be avoided, future aspects of a life that no psychic should ascertain—otherwise, experiences that were meant for a soul's progress would be either avoided or approached in a different manner.

There are times when the psychic advice I have to offer seems almost ambiguous—a cop-out. When I was in Japan giving psychic consultations at a Buddhist monastery, the mother of the head priest asked for a reading. There were many questions on her mind, but none as important as that regarding her son.

"Can you tell this lady when her son is going to be married?" my interpreter, Ryuske Tokunaga, translated. "She is much concerned, as he is getting on in years and it is important to her that he marry and have children."

I was in a semi-trance at the time—quite easy to achieve in the contemplative, peaceful, wondrously spiritual atmosphere of the monastery. Closing my eyes, the thought came to me that he would not ever be married in this life. And I had another impression that I was not to say this to the mother.

We were sitting opposite each other on the tatami mat on the floor, and I reached out and touched the arm of this lovely, fragile woman in the simple kimono. As I did, thoughts from my subconscious were quickly formulated into words. "You are not to worry about this. When and if the time is right, your son will be married; not before, not after. It is not for you to be concerned."

I waited as Ryuske translated my words, expecting the worst. Had this seemingly ambiguous prophecy been told to anyone in my own country, I most certainly would have been asked for an exact time of the marriage or been accused of hedging the issue. In fact, had I been the one asking the question, I don't believe I would have been satisfied with that answer, so I expected some sort of reproach.

Instead, she looked at me, smiled, and then began to cry. I was startled. Then the lovely lady regained her composure and quietly spoke to Ryuske. He told me she said my answer to her had truly been that of a Buddhist. The answer had been sufficient, complete, and very meaningful to her, apparently on many levels.

It took me a moment to realize that this woman's culture had been steeped in psychical and spiritual awareness for centuries. Therefore, the immediate response from my subconscious was the correct one for her. She was not to be afforded even the comfort that her son would be married. The approach to their karma together was in her *not* knowing, at least at that time. She understood the reading.

In this particular instance, I couldn't control words which came from within. The question was asked, and the psychic answer was there, quite independently. The words formed in my mind as I spoke them. There was no question of deciding what I was to say.

There are times when this lack of control of a prophetic statement I have made has gotten me into difficulty. When I was a youth it was most disconcerting and often disastrous when I "spoke before thinking" (something I have often been accused of doing) and my words later proved to have a direct effect on the one to whom I addressed them.

I had a few close chums in high school on Long Island.

One, named Frank, was quite adult for his age. He had a good after-school job as an automobile mechanic, and most of our friends looked up to him as a mature, well-developed person.

Frank was in love with a girl who attended a neighboring school. Their relationship had started when they were both in grade school, and as soon as they graduated high school, they planned to be married. One day Frank and I were discussing his forthcoming marriage, which he and Ann had planned for June, several months ahead.

"I've already made arrangements to start on a permanent basis with my job," Frank told me. "I'd like you to be my best man. Ann's going to work for a cousin of hers who owns a dress shop."

As he spoke, I became very uncomfortable. At first I brushed this negative feeling aside. I was not consciously utilizing any psychic abilities at that time; in fact I didn't even know what they were.

"I'd love to be best man for you some day, Frank," I said without any thought to what I was saying.

"*Some* day? I just told you that we have the date set for June 27," Frank said.

"Maybe when she comes back . . ." I stopped, not knowing why I had said *that*.

"What the hell are you talking about?" Frank was getting angry that I wasn't listening to him.

"Oh, I don't know," I answered him. "I don't think Ann will be here in June." I was really puzzled now. Why was I saying such a dumb thing?

"This is crazy; you don't know what you're talking about."

But the next statement just spewed from my mouth. "You won't marry Ann, not just now, maybe later." For the first time, I realized that I couldn't have controlled my words had my life depended on it.

"Dammit!" Frank shouted, slamming down his books on the table in the school library where we had been having the conversation, "you're really weird, you know?"

"Yeah, I guess so," I said, now confused and embarrassed at having spoken before I knew what I was talking about.

"Really weird," Frank repeated, quite upset and angry. He picked up his books and left me at the table. I didn't try to follow him and explain that I had no control over the words. He would not have understood. I didn't understand it myself.

About a month later I heard that Ann's father had died suddenly of a heart attack. Her mother had decided to go back to Minnesota immediately to live with her family. It was all very unexpected, and since Ann was quite close to her father, the experience had been quite devastating to her. She told Frank that she had to go with her mother. "I'll be back when I can," Ann had explained. "I love you, Frank, but there's nothing I can do. My mother feels that she has to go, and I've got to be with her for a little while. When things are settled with her and the family, I'll be back."

Ann returned in the fall of that year, but she and Frank never did get married. I think that Frank never forgave her for leaving when she did, and that a feeling of trust disappeared when she left for Minnesota.

And speaking of trust, Frank broke off the friendship with me. He intimated that the day I told him he wouldn't be marrying Ann that June, I knew more about the situation than I had let on. He felt that there was some kind of conspiracy, that possibly other persons knew that Ann was trying to get out of the situation and simply used the excuse of her father's death to break the relationship.

This was nonsense, of course. I had met Ann only twice. I did not know anything about her parents; her father was not ill before he had the heart attack. There was no physical evidence that Frank and Ann would not marry that June. Their plans were set, firm, and unchangeable, at least in their own minds. But something in my conversation with Frank triggered the psychic response I gave him.

As a child I loved motion pictures and spent many an evening with my mother at the local theater. It seemed that I somehow knew certain things about the characters or plot that would come up later in the film. I'd proceed to tell my mother the outcome of certain plot situations or character developments during the film.

"Can't you keep that mouth of yours quiet?" my mother would often say to me in the darkened movie house. She never could figure out how I knew the outcome of so many of these films.

To a degree, I learned to hold back my speech before thinking, but there have been many occasions when I could not. The sentences just rolled out before I could stop them.

As a hopeful actor in my early twenties, I lost many friends when I'd tell them not to waste time going to auditions for an acting job they particularly wanted. I became known in some theatrical circles as the jinx—a reaction that is often the bane of a psychic's existence. There are persons who believe that a psychic causes the outcome of a situation that he has prophesied instead of merely sensing the way it will turn out. Ah, if I but had *that* talent I'd be in control of the world by now!

I have had arguments with persons who have come to me for psychic advice and then turned on me during the reading, denying that what I told them could even have the slightest possibility of occurring.

"Will I marry Robert?" one well-known society matron asked me recently during a psychic consultation.

"No," I answered.

"I will too! How dare you tell me this? We are in love. I wanted your psychic confirmation. We're engaged."

The lady was outraged. She had come to receive confirmation of something she felt to be a fact, and I had given her the opposite of what she wished to hear.

"I just don't see you married," I said, when I could get a word in edgewise over her by now almost indecent barrage of words.

"I will be married to him!"

"Then if you already know, why ask me? Don't you think it's a waste of time, effort, and money to ask something you already positively know?"

"All I know is that I will marry him," she repeated again.

She did indeed marry Robert. However, the marriage lasted only three weeks. Had she not verbally attacked me, I might possibly have been able to elaborate on the matter during the consultation. The fact was that I did not see them married.

The same thing happened when I gave a number of predictions for the upcoming year of 1972 to the *Albany* [New York] *Times-Union.* I felt that Nixon would win the election, but I did not see Spiro Agnew as vice-president. I sensed a different man altogether. At that time it was an odd prediction.

"Can you elaborate on this?" Virginia Spain Spring, the reporter interviewing me, asked.

"Not really. I just don't see him with Nixon."

When I first tuned into the elections, I saw Nixon but could not get any image of his running mate. I just knew that Agnew would not be vice-president of the United States. Some people, including those in the media, took this to mean that Agnew would not be on the ticket with Nixon.

Interpretation is sometimes impossible when there are so many possibilities in any given situation.

I have often spoken before thinking, and not until recently was it brought to my attention that the word "prophecy" is from the Greek "prophetia," which means "speaking before." To me a prophet is thus one who speaks before attempting to analyze or interpret to any given situation the immediate psychic response he receives. A prophet is one who speaks before contemplating not only the outcome of a situation but very often the situation itself.

"Who will win this year's Academy Award for best actress?" I was asked on a TV show in 1969.

"It will either be Barbra Streisand or Katherine Hepburn," I replied.

"You've got to be more specific than that," was the demand.

"I can't seem to narrow it down. It will be either one of those two," was the only honest reply I could give.

"Well, there are five actresses nominated, and you've given us two. That doesn't seem too difficult."

"I guess it means that it will be very close," I said sheepishly, realizing that the answer hadn't been sufficient for the skeptical man placing me on the firing line.

"I wouldn't call that a prophecy, then, even if one of them did win." His statement was curt and meant to demolish.

To my own astonishment, as well as that of the rest of the world, when the Academy Award winners were announced for 1969, *both* Katherine Hepburn and Barbra Streisand had won, splitting the votes directly down the middle. This was the first time that the Best Actress award had been given to two people.

I had not seen the outcome of the situation, nor the possibility of two people winning. However, I could not narrow it down to one person because my psychic impression was of both actresses. I did not know that there could even be a tie in this situation. The prediction was correct, even if the interpretation left a lot to be desired.

Jeanne McDowell is an opera singer and a teacher of music from near Rochester, New York. She came to me for a consultation in 1970, seeking psychic advice on her life, her family, and business. Her husband owned and operated a sand quarry.

"What can you tell me of my husband?" she asked. "He has not been too well of late."

"Do you want the truth, the complete truth?" I asked, hoping that she would want to have nothing hidden from her.

"Naturally," she said, quite taken aback. "Who would come to you expecting to hear anything but what you do psychically feel?"

"A lot of people," I replied, "and quite often."

"Well, I'd like to know exactly what it is you feel."

"I do think that you must make plans to carry on without your husband. If you prepare yourself for the worst, you and your children will not be hurt. I do not see your husband here after next year." I cringed at having given her this prediction, but my psychic impression was that the man had no chance of survival and that she ought to know.

"You have confirmed what I have thought myself," Mrs. McDowell said. "And I'm glad you told me, because there is a great deal that I must do to get things in order. On an unconscious level I have felt that my husband would die, but I've put off facing it. I'm grateful for the confirmation you have given me, even though it is most distressing." Mrs. McDowell's husband did die, but she had prepared herself for the ordeal and she was able to surmount this difficult time because of her preparation.

I find that about half of my work is in the confirmation of certain future events that a person already knows, whether it be on a conscious or an unconscious level. This aspect of my work involves not only prophecy, but telepathy as well.

Al is a young man who ran an antique shop near where I live. He began asking me for some psychic advice about his business.

I told him my impressions and then said, "But you had better get things in order, because I sense travel for you. In fact, I am sensing you in a foreign place, most probably India. You will be in India before the year is out."

Al looked at me quizzically and a bit astonished. "My wife and I talked about that for some time about six months ago. Being students of Meher Baba, we've recently had a desire to visit India. You must have been mind reading."

"You will go," I said again.

"No way!" Al was adamant. "We don't have the money right now for any sort of trip."

"The way will open up for you. You will be able to go, and I feel that you must if the opportunity comes."

Al was quick to recall one of my cardinal rules dealing with giving persons prophecies. "I thought you never made choices for people."

"I don't, unless it's for some sort of soul progress. I feel that this will be your last chance to get over there for some time, and if you hold yourself back from going, it could be very negative. In this instance, I do see the outcome of the situation if you don't go—regret and sorrow."

"Well, it doesn't have a chance of happening anyway. I'm thousands of dollars in debt just now."

I told him to wait and see.

Months later, Al's wife received some money from a recently deceased relative. It was a total surprise to Al's wife, who did not know her relative had any money at all. The couple talked it over to decide what should be done with it—the bills, repairs on the house, or a trip to India. They decided to go to India.

Upon their arrival back in the States, they visited me. They had almost not gone, but could not get the fact out of their heads that I had foreseen this opportunity to go to India. They decided that I also might have been right in saying that they had better go at that time.

While in India, Al and his wife had many experiences pertaining to spiritual enlightenment. One of the more positive ones was the ability to go into meditation without the use of drugs (marijuana, mushrooms, etc.), something they had been interested in before the Indian enlightenment journey.

Within a few months after their return, Al's wife became pregnant, and he decided to go into the real estate business with a relative. Although he is a successful man at present, his work keeps him on the go six days a week, and he agrees that he wouldn't have been able to visit India had he not gone at the time he did.

In this case I had confirmed something they had already talked about and desired but put out of the mind due to circumstances. This confirmation of things already sensed in the prophecy I gave them had been the deciding factor in their going to India, placing faith in what I foresaw would be the outcome if they did not go.

Psychic confirmation is an important part of any psychic's work, yet to the skeptical or the uninitiated, it is not as dramatic or seemingly "prophetic" as when a correct prediction sees fruition against current belief and great odds.

In 1972 I lectured for the Spiritual Frontiers Fellowship in Rochester, New York. I returned for a second lecture there in 1974. Both occasions gave me the opportunity to give many psychic readings. The aforementioned Jeanne McDowell was one, as was Ellen Smith, whose daughter was attending college in California in 1972.

"I'd like to know whether my daughter will remain in California or teach in New Mexico when she gets out of school," Mrs. Smith asked.

"Neither," I replied.

She appeared puzzled. "What did you say?"

"She will not teach in either California or New Mexico. I psychically sense her close to home. For one reason or another, your daughter will return to Rochester and teach in a local school here."

Mrs. Smith was not only surprised but a bit alarmed by the prophecy. "This is impossible. She doesn't like this area, and she has no intentions whatsoever of returning. Her desire is to teach at either of two schools, which she has already applied for, in both the states I mentioned."

I could sense that she had become uncomfortable, questioning whether I was really psychic. She had offered me the required factual information, and I had vetoed both choices, giving her a third alternative which she had not even contemplated.

I didn't sense the daughter anywhere else. "She will be back in this area," I repeated.

"I'd like to believe that," she said slowly, "but this time I think you're wrong."

When I returned to Rochester in 1974, I was greeted by Mrs. Smith who immediately told me that her daughter had indeed returned to Rochester and was happily teaching at a local school. It had been the furthest thing from the consciousness of anyone concerned in the matter. Even Mr. Smith, most skeptical in regard to psychical pronouncements, could not comprehend the way in which I had ascertained the correct prophetic information I had given his wife.

During a delicious dinner his wife had prepared, Mr. Smith asked me how I knew his daughter would return. But my only answer was to say I just knew. This "just knowing" something to be a fact is the best way I can describe the process I go through when a prophetic feeling flashes across my mind.

Recently, I was again afforded the confirmation of the outcome of a situation I foresaw which, when initially stated, received a negative response. I had been in Orlando, Florida, addressing the Spiritual Research Society of Orlando and giving psychic readings. A year later I received a letter from a Ms. Sandra Helton. Herewith is the exact content of the letter's third paragraph:

Of the predictions you made while here, one in particular that has unfolded was of interest to me. The evening before you left, you saw a young woman who had learned that her brother had only a few weeks to live. She later told me that she had been made most upset by you because you told her that there was nothing wrong with her brother and had refused to change what you saw even though she insisted on what the doctors had definitely stated, which was that he had a terminal condition in the brain. A couple of months ago while I was visiting a friend who is an art therapist in the hospital where the girl is a nurse, I saw her and was compelled to ask about her brother. He *is* well, and it seems that further examination revealed that he did not have this brain condition and the doctors have never been able to explain what had happened to him.

In the case of this prophecy, which does involve telecommunication, I was able to sense the eventual well-being of the girl's brother. When his sister initially asked me about the brain condition, I sensed nothing in his aura that would indicate this kind of disease. He would be well despite his sister's insistence that he was to die within a short period of time. I knew that she did not believe me, that she felt I was only attempting to make her feel good by not telling her of his eventual demise. My refusal to change the prophecy infuriated her, since all the evidence was against my feeling.

There are many who will seek out psychic advice and then pick and choose what they feel can fit certain known conditions around them. I find this a bit strange, especially since they have come with the realization that dealing with the unknown factors in situations is what a psychic does in the first place.

TWO

Elizabethan ESP

Recently, I had the opportunity to see once again *Throne of Blood,* the Japanese film version of Shakespeare's *Macbeth.* I was a bit taken aback by the approach to the story, for the director, Akira Kurosawa, gave the motion picture many overtones of the mystical and supernatural, which were missing or merely hinted at in any of the productions of the play I had seen before.

It dawned on me that this Japanese interpretation was probably more accurate than any productions performed in our Western culture, which tend to underplay the aura of the occult and the prophetic atmosphere which in truth permeate the writing of *Macbeth.*

There is little dispute that William Shakespeare was one of the greatest writers who ever lived. His works are the most valid, human, and important documents that any one man has yet produced. Through the centuries, Shakespeare's works have been interpreted and analyzed

21

by thousands of critics, psychologists, artists, cler-
gymen—by members of any professional field one might
care to mention. His writings touched on every conceiva-
ble aspect of the behavior of man and are as meaningful
now as they were when they were written almost four
hundred years ago. One need read nothing else in a
lifetime but Shakespeare's works to glean a complete
material and spiritual evolvement and understanding,
and indeed, I have chosen to refer to Shakespeare's
works throughout the rest of this book.

It is odd that few who have been involved in the occult
and the supernatural have bothered to delve into the
works of Shakespeare. Indeed, many critics throughout
the ages have stated that Shakespeare merely pandered
to his era's popular superstitious beliefs and customs. It
is my belief, however, that Shakespeare placed great faith
in the ghosts, witches, demons, spirits, trances, and
prophecies that he so frequently wove into his plays.

The extent to which Shakespeare did believe in the
supernatural is evident in almost all of his writings. In
order to have written many of his plays, an understanding of the occult sciences was not only necessary but
inevitable. Without this understanding, few of his plays
would exist. Even Act I, Scene II, of the outwardly political *Antony and Cleopatra* contains a hilarious sequence in
which a palmist tries vainly to get an important reading
across to two scatterbrained girls in Cleopatra's retinue.
This scene shows not just an awareness of the occult, but
how it usually operates in the everyday world.

Again, there are those who feel that Shakespeare's
continuous excursions into the realms of the supernatural was for the sole purpose of bringing about some
dramatic stage effects. But I feel that his constant delv-
ings into the supernatural world give real clues to his
mind, affording deeper significance to these so-called
"stage devices." Of course Shakespeare's ghostly apparitions, the practice of magic, the prophetic statements,

the witches and the other supernatural elements he wrote about were indeed a reflection of his era—the supernatural was then, for the most part, unthinkingly accepted; today the supernatural aspects of Shakespeare's writings are usually rejected by a society that has become jaded and sated with an overabundancy of scientific data and intellectualism.

It has been written by most of Shakespeare's critics and by historians as well, that this great writer went to extremes in order to hide his own personal views and beliefs in his plays. They usually say that he strove to utilize a universality in his works rather than taking a personalized, objective stand. This theory has persisted through the centuries because of the idolatry of which Shakespeare has indeed been the victim. The theory makes him very impersonal, aloof from any other artist who has ever created. The critics have divested him of almost any human qualities, preferring to believe that he possessed some unnatural kind of genius and that his writings somehow came down to him in computerized form from a higher plane of existence. The very human qualities that we have come to honor and cherish in Shakespeare's works are usually not attributed to the man himself.

As John Ruskin said, "Let a man hide himself from you everywhere, yet in his work he is bound to be revealed." This goes tenfold for any creative work an artist may be involved in. Only now, at the dawning of the age of Aquarius, are we able to realize that what Shakespeare wrote about concerned his own thoughts—very possibly brought to his consciousness while in a state of meditation, yet *his* thoughts, *his* beliefs, *his* awareness.

It is no coincidence that Shakespeare's writings have always been reinterpreted, reevaluated, in direct ratio to the philosophical, spiritual, and overall advancement of any given era. We have always taken what was needed and understood from his works at different periods in our history. For example, Sigmund Freud presented completely new insights into the works of Shakespeare by utilizing psychoanalytical methods to discover how and why Shakespeare's characters acted as they did. His theory of Hamlet and the Oedipus complex is but one of the many insights offered us by one great man interpreting the works of another. Now, in this new age of enlightenment, it is time to reevaluate and utilize what Shakespeare wrote in regard to the occult and the supernatural.

Reading Shakespeare's plays in the probable order in which they were written, we discover that there were several marked changes in his personal beliefs. Shakespeare's writings when he was a wayward, spirited youth who was often struck with hard, bitter times, reflect his materialistic attitudes, his sensualism. He comes through as one who is absorbed in the purely physical aspects of life. These early plays reflect the material beauty, romanticism, color, and exuberance of life that was Shakespeare in his youth.

Sir Sidney Lee* concluded that the works through Shakespeare's middle and later years "must be judged to reflect his personal feelings."

In the plays of his later years, Shakespeare wrote about the supernatural more often than not. It is in *Hamlet* that Shakespeare first created a theme that depended on the influence over a mortal being—young Hamlet—by an "entity" from beyond—his father's ghost. *Hamlet* marks a concise stage in Shakespeare's mental and spiritual awareness and development. His remaining plays progressively take on subjects relating to the occult—the witches, ghosts, demons, persons possessed, prophecies, and other forms of the outer realms of existence—especially his serious works.

---

* 1859–1926, author of *The Life of Shakespeare* (1891).

The supernatural becomes the main theme of what most historians have thought of as Shakespeare's final work, *The Tempest.* In this play, Shakespeare presents his view that the material world is but a passing delusion, merely a mask through which man catches quick glimpses of peaceful, eternal reality which shall endure forever when the physical has passed away.

In many of the speeches of Prospero, Shakespeare made clear his own beliefs regarding the occult. Prospero has turned his back on the material world, detesting its pomp and vanities. He has found that he can control not only those around him (Caliban, his slave, and Ariel, his obedient spirit), but the very elements of the earth, the currents of the air, and the waves in the ocean.

In one particular speech, Prospero expresses what I believe to be Shakespeare's own later philosophy of life, his personal outlook which had become mature and which had brought serenity into his life:

> *These our actors,*
> *As I foretold you, were all spirits, and*
> *Are melted into air, into thin air:*
> *And, like the baseless fabric of this vision,*
> *The cloud-clapp'd towers, the gorgeous palaces,*
> *The solemn temples, the great globe itself,*
> *Yea, all which it inherit, shall dissolve,*
> *And, like this insubstantial pageant faded,*
> *Leave not a rack behind. We are such stuff*
> *As dreams are made on, and our little life*
> *Is rounded with a sleep.*

Shakespeare came to believe that matter is ultimately an illusion and that only mind is reality. There is a unifying thread throughout all his plays, a searching for the truth of what reality is and what it is not.

It was in *Hamlet* that Shakespeare first began to delve deeply into the supernatural and question the material

world. One speech which Hamlet gives is indeed Shakespeare himself starting his own personal quest into the
realms of the other world:

> To die, to sleep;
> To sleep: perchance to dream: ay, there's the rub;
> For in that sleep of death what dreams may come
> When we have shuffled off this mortal coil,
> Must give us pause.

It is ironic that it has taken three centuries for man to
recognize that the entire question of the true origin of
man and his destiny rests upon the issues that Shakespeare raised.

Over and over again, throughout most of his plays,
Shakespeare reveals his belief in the hereafter and the
spiritual aspects of life, and this is never more apparent
than in these words spoken in *Macbeth:*

> Life's but a walking shadow, a poor player
> That struts and frets his hour upon the stage,
> And then is heard no more: it is a tale
> Told by an idiot, full of sound and fury,
> Signifying nothing.

It is in this same play that much of Shakespeare's feelings about the supernatural are brought into focus. It is
a work which delves deeply into the mystery of a positive
supernatural energy versus a negative supernatural
energy. Prophecy plays a most important role in this play
as it does in *Julius Caesar, Romeo and Juliet,* and several
others.

The witches in *Macbeth* who prophesied are not merely
Elizabethan old hags brought into the action to create
a certain atmosphere and spectacle, as a vast number of
Shakespeare's more "intellectual" critics have charged.
Macbeth *believes* in the power of the three weird sisters.

Through them, he makes a pact with a negative psychic energy. In Macbeth's first meeting with the witches they prophesy that he will be the Thane of Cawder:

> *All hail, Macbeth! hail to thee, Thane of Cawder!*
> *All hail, Macbeth! that shalt be king hereafter!*

Macbeth knows that the Thane of Cawder is living and demands to know from "whence you owe this strange intelligence." He also immediately asks why the sisters have stopped him on "this blasted heath . . . with such prophetic greeting."

Banquo, who is with Macbeth, wonders if they had in truth seen the three sisters or "have we eaten on the insane root that takes the reason prisoner?" (an illusion to a hallucinatory herb). Macbeth is immediately taken in by their prophecy that he will be king and from the outset shows no sign of questioning their existence. He bemoans their initial disappearance: "Would they have stayed!"

Later, Macbeth demands to see the future in the witches' cave and then is quite prepared to meet the witches' "masters." He does not seem afraid, although he is aware that he has made a serious step in challenging the witches, in demanding that they tell him more.

In the first act, Macbeth is quite dazzled by the prophecy and the elusive quality of the witches. By the third act, he fully realizes that in seeking out the prophetesses, he is completely committing himself to an evil, supernatural force.

> *More shall they speak; for now I am bent to know,*
> *By the worst means, the worst. For mine own good*
> *All causes shall give way . . .*

Macbeth knows that the witches embody a force that is against all moral order and decency:

I conjure you, by that which you profess
(Howe'er you come to know it) answer me:
Though you untie the winds and let them fight
Against the churches; though the yesty waves
Confound and swallow navigation up;
Though bladed corn be lodged and trees blown down;
Though castles topple on their warders' heads;
Though palaces and pyramids do slope
Their heads to their foundations; though the treasure
Of Nature's germens tumble all together,
Even till destruction sicken; answer me
To what I ask you.

The preceding passage proves Shakespeare's understanding of the workings of black magic: that in order to use such an energy, some kind of sacrifice must be made. Macbeth commands the witches to answer his questioning about the future at any cost to himself and the world around him.

The great contrast in *Macbeth* comes into play with the link by Macbeth's adversaries with a positive psychic energy—as pitted against his own pact made with a negative supernatural energy. Duncan is referred to throughout the play as a goodly king, "a most sainted king." The entire passage on the king's ability to heal the sick and of his "heavenly gift of prophecy" is much more than a placating compliment passed off onto King James I, who ruled during Shakespeare's later years and who was said to possess these same spiritual qualities.

It is exciting to read the lines in Act IV, Scene III, that make reference to the spiritual gifts of Edward, King of England. Macduff has fled England to join forces with Malcolm against Macbeth:

Enter a Doctor
MALCOLM [to the doctor]: . . . Comes the king
                 forth, I pray you?

DOCTOR: Ay, sir; there are a crew of wretched souls
                 That stay his cure; their malady convinces

> The great assay of art; but, *at his touch,*
> Such sanctity hath heaven given his hand,
> They presently amend.

The doctor then exits, and Malcolm and Macduff continue the conversation they were having before the medic's intrusion. Macduff, a bit confused, asks Malcolm what manner of disease it is that King Edward can cure. Malcolm replies that the king can cure what " 'Tis called the evil." He goes on to tell of the miraculous work in the art of psychic healing he has seen the king perform since escaping to England:

> How *he solicits heaven,*
> *Himself best knows: but strangely-visited people,*
> *All swoln and ulcerous, pitiful to the eye,*
> *The mere despair of surgery, he cures* . . .

The three sisters also prophesied that Banquo's heirs shall rule. King James I, Shakespeare's king, was a direct descendant of Banquo. It is significant that this parallel of King Edward's miracles as opposed to the prophecies of the sisters is passed down on both sides to future generations. A balance of these opposing energies is thus created by the witches' "unlawful" prophecy that the heirs of Banquo will rule—as against the miraculous prophecy of the "healing benediction" which is passed onto Edward's successors to the throne.

The raging battle of these positive supernatural forces against the negative is the foundation to the entire structure of *Macbeth.* It is most disquieting, therefore, to read the analyses of even the most august of Shakespeare's advocates who continually state that if the witches' scenes were eliminated, the play would remain the same!

It is just as disconcerting to see productions of *Macbeth* that utilize vastly exaggerated effects whenever the sisters are on stage. A more truthful approach would be to have the sisters appear simply as three prophetesses, dressed in costumes of the day—merely psychic women who prophesy for Macbeth. All the mist and haze that arise from cauldrons filled with dry ice is not only ludicrous but is not, I feel, what Shakespeare had in mind.

My psychic impression is that Shakespeare based the three sisters on those who were involved in witchcraft and black magic, possibly Druids. The three sisters can thus be looked upon as being members of a coven or a cult, of which there were many in Macbeth's era. I believe that Hecate, who confronts the sisters during the play in great anger because they have not consulted her before giving their prophecies to Macbeth, is the leader of this cult or coven. It is quite apparent when Hecate waits for the sisters and meets them on the heath:

> FIRST WITCH: Why, how now, Hecate! You look angerly.
>
> HECATE: Have I not reason, beldams as you
>   are,
>   Saucy and overbold? How did you dare
>   To trade and traffic with Macbeth
>   In riddles and affairs of death;
>   And I, *the mistress of your charms,**
>   The close contriver of all harms,
>   Was never call'd to bear my part,
>   Or show the glory of our art?

Interesting is the fact that Shakespeare chose to name the leader of the sisters Hecate, as this namesake appears in many stories of old and is in reference to the goddess of the moon, earth, and underworld—the ruler of all demons and witches.

The entire action of *Macbeth* hinges on the prophecies of the three sisters. They are true prophecies, given to Macbeth as any modern-day psychic might repeat them. However, Macbeth grossly misinterprets them. Once

* Italics authors.

again, the problem of the correct interpretation of a prophecy, this time in fictionalized form, is made manifest.

Macbeth believes the three sisters because he wants to believe them, of course, but also because they had correctly prophesied for him earlier when they hailed him Thane of Cawder before he was thus named by his king. I believe that the prophecies given to Macbeth by the psychic-apparitions which are conjured by the sisters is the *raison d'être* for *Macbeth*'s being written at all. Through the ages, as we became more scientific and more intellectual and downgraded prophecy, witchcraft, and the supernatural, many scholars decided that the witches and their prophecies were incidental to the plot. Let me repeat, *there is no plot without them.*

In the witches' care the apparitions appear most symbolically to Macbeth, but in his egotistical arrogance he is unable to accept what is psychically manifested before him. The first apparition (that of an armed head) offers Macbeth fair warning of his enemy:

> *Macbeth! Macbeth! Macbeth! beware Macduff,*
> *Beware the thane of Fife.*

The second apparition (that of a bloody child) tells Macbeth to:

> *Be bloody, bold, and resolute: laugh to scorn*
> *The power of man; for none of woman born*
> *Shall harm Macbeth.*

Macbeth rationalizes that Macduff must have been born of woman and decides not to accept this prophetic warning: "Then live, Macduff: what need I fear of thee?"

By the time the third apparition appears (that of a child with a tree in its hand) Macbeth is convinced that no harm can come to him from Macduff. This misinterpreted prophecy convinces Macbeth that he is safe:

Macbeth shall never vanquished be until
Great Birnam wood to high Dunsinane hill
Shall come against him.

Macbeth interprets this prophecy literally, believing that it means he can be conquered only when the Birnam forest becomes uprooted and marches against him. With but a bit more insight, Macbeth might have "seen" that the child holding the tree in its hand was a direct vision of his enemies who would in reality march against him beneath *branches* of the Birnam trees, which they utilized as a sort of camouflage.

At the end of the play, it is made clear that Macduff was "from his mother's womb untimely ripped." Thus the prophecy that "none of woman born shall harm Macbeth" in its correct interpretation is a truthful one. The sisters have not lied to Macbeth nor tricked him. He has tricked himself by allowing his ego to misinterpret the prophecies.

In *Macbeth*, Shakespeare was trying to show us the effects on persons who utilize a negative psychic energy. As in most instances of such utilization, Macbeth was offered much for making such a pact. He went far. In the end, however, he was done in by the very psychic energy he sought to harness. This aspect of evil power destroying whoever makes a bond with it was the basis of my book *America Bewitched.**

Macbeth has given up all honor, loyalty, friendship, and morality for his ambition, placing his entire faith in the sisters' prophecies. This element is much more than merely atmosphere, for every action shows the temporary control of evil energies over the outline of things. Again and again, Shakespeare makes the point that under very particular conditions favorable to evil, the mind of man can be not only influenced, but overtaken, by exterior spirit energies or entities.

* New York: William Morrow, 1974.

A mood of negative psychic energy pervades the entire action of *Macbeth,* constantly being observed and commented on by most of the play's characters. It is Macbeth, however, who is most sensitive to it, most willing to accept it. Macbeth seems to understand the very mood of specific places and the exact times of the day when the powers of this negative energy, this evil, are in the ascendant. Just before the two murders, he explains his feeling of unity with these unnatural psychic forces, which in turn afford him support and strength:

> *Now o'er the one half-world*
> *Nature seems dead, and wicked dreams abuse*
> *The curtain'd sleep; Witchcraft celebrates*
> *Pale Hecate's off'rings.*

This same feeling of a pact with evil comes when Macbeth sends the murderers to kill Banquo. It is not until the final effrontery that Macbeth throws off his faith in the prophecies of the sisters and decides to fight Macduff.

King John is a historical play by Shakespeare that I had not read or seen performed, but I came upon it one day while doing research. It is a play of political intrigue and religious pageantry: King John is pitted against the Papal state. In Act IV, Scene II, Philip Faulconbridge, the bastard son of King Richard I, appears before King John. He has with him Peter of Pomfret, a prophet. According to the sixteenth-century historian Raphael Holinshed, Peter of Pomfret was "in great reputation with the common people for his predictions."

> PHILIP [to King John]: How I have sped among
> the clergymen,
> The sums I have collected shall express.
> But as I travail'd hither through the land,
> I find the people strangely fantasied;
> Possess'd with rumours, full of idle
> dreams,

> Not knowing what they fear, but full of
> fear.
> And here's a prophet that I brought with
> me
> From forth the streets of Pomfret, whom
> I found
> With many hundreds treading on his
> heals;
> To whom he sung, in rude harsh-sound-
> ing rimes,
> That, ere the next Ascension-day at noon,
> Your highness should deliver up your
> crown.

KING JOHN: Thou idle dreamer, wherefore dids't thou
             so?

PETER: Foreknowing that the truth will fall out
             so.

KING JOHN: Hubert, away with him; imprison him;
             And on that day at noon, whereon he says
             I shall yield up my crown, let him be
             hang'd.

Holinshed informs us that on the next Ascension Day,
1213, "the day passed without any seeming damage unto
King John, and Peter of Pomfret was dragged behind
horses through the streets of Wareham and hanged until
dead." His innocent son was also hanged at the same
time, apparently for nothing more than having the ill
luck to be the heir of the prophet.

In *King John*, as in the writings of Holinshed and other
historians, it is quite clear that Peter's prophecy was fulfilled. But his words were in need of interpretation, again
proving that Shakespeare knew much about the inner
workings of the occult. It was on this same Ascension Day
that King John was made to pay homage to the Pope, for
England had become a Papal fief against John's wishes.
Thus, the prophecy that King John would have to deliver

up his crown takes on an even deeper significance than if he had lost it to some usurper or in battle.

Again the theme of a correct prophecy being given an incorrect interpetation comes into play. As in *Julius Caesar* and *Macbeth,* this incorrect understanding led to bloodshed and dire consequences. Prophecies are to be taken seriously and carefully meditated upon, not taken at face value, but rather thought over for any deeper meaning they might hold for the one receiving their predictive nature.

The prophecies in *King John* are as meaningful and important to the plot as the prophetic dreams of Calpurnia and the predictive mouthings of the soothsayer in *Julius Caesar,* or the manifestations of the spirit body of the old King in *Hamlet.* At this stage of our evolution, we should be able to interpret Shakespeare's constant allusions to the supernatural world as more than being merely the devices of a brilliant playwright. For, as Hamlet says to Horatio, "There are more things in heaven and earth than are dreamt of in your philosophy."

THREE

Omens, Emotions, and Need

Elsie Sechrist's home is located in a suburb of Houston, Texas. The house, filled with peaceful, quiet, good vibrations, reflects the fine taste of this most respected woman, who in the area of dream interpretation has made an enlightening contribution to the world of parapsychology.

In March of 1969 I was in Houston completing an extensive thirteen-city promotional tour in connection with my autobiography. I had spent the entire day making television and radio appearances, plus a newspaper interview with Anna Miller of the *Houston Chronicle.*

I had not met Mrs. Sechrist previously, but she had heard of my visit to Houston via an early-morning radio interview I had, and somehow she managed to trace me down at another station before my appearance on the air. I was more than happy to accept her kind invitation to attend a small dinner party in my honor that evening. It

37

would be a chance for me to get some sorely needed rest and also to meet others interested in the more spiritual realms of the occult. Anna Miller, who was an acquaintance of Mrs. Sechrist, was also invited. A few other friends had been asked as well, ones whom Mrs. Sechrist knew would not tax me more than necessary. When the word gets around a gathering that there is a "real live psychic" in their midst, I am usually asked to "perform" some magical, mystical, psychic feat—even after a full day's schedule of radio and TV interviews.

Mrs. Sechrist fully realized the energy and strength, both physical and spiritual, necessary for one to do a promotional tour, having recently toured herself in connection with her best seller, *Dreams: Your Magic Mirror.**

After an excellent dinner we retired to the living room for a drink and some talk. Anna Miller showed interest in the recent upheaval that Bishop James Pike had created in the Episcopal Church. His investigations into the world of psychic phenomena had stirred much antagonism against him by those in the hierarchy of the Church, especially since he was attempting to communicate with the dead. He had received national media coverage when he attended seances held by world famous medium, Arthur Ford, and was convinced that Ford had been able to contact the spirit of his son Jim, who had committed suicide some time before. This was proving to be the last straw for his superiors in the Church.

Although we had the same publisher at that time, I had never met or talked with Bishop Pike.

"What do you get psychically on Bishop Pike?" Anna Miller asked me. "I mean, will he be asked to step down from his role as Bishop, or what?"

When at first I did not answer her, Anna Miller repeated her question. I had had an instant, overpowering feeling of foreboding in regard to Pike. I closed my eyes

* New York: Cowles, 1968.

and there was only a deep, black void. The flesh on my skin crawled. This feeling of an emptiness and physical trembling usually symbolizes a death in my consciousness.

Mrs. Miller asked if I had heard her.

"Bishop Pike doesn't have a future," I said. "Before the next six to eight months, he will join his son in death. It might be a suicide."

Those in the room fell silent. The prophecy had come forth very unexpectedly, so forcefully that it shocked even me. Mrs. Miller was simply asking what I felt his future status in the Church would be, and I had come forth with a prediction of tragedy and death. I try not to give prophecies concerning death, even when I receive them quite strongly, and in this instance I became angry with myself.

The subject was soon changed and the party eventually came to an end. The next day I was off to another city, but I still felt odd about the prediction I had made concerning Bishop Pike. Every time I tried to meditate or tune into his vibrations, this overpowering feeling of death filled my being. Realizing that Bishop Pike and I were writing books for the same publisher, I did call my editor at the time. But I could only tell him of my feeling. He didn't seem to think there was anything he could do. It was most frustrating.

At about this same time in 1969 I had purchased a home in the Catskill Mountain region of New York. The house, although small, met all my needs; it was away from the negative vibrations of New York City, off by itself where I would go to rejuvenate myself, regain my energies, and be able to write. I had made a few friends in my new location, and one of them was a young man named Christopher. Throughout the spring of 1969 I worked on the house, hoping to get it ready for a housewarming in the fall, and Christopher was most kind in assisting me in this redecorating job.

It was now a hot, humid August day, the air stifling and muggy. Christopher and I had worked on the house the entire morning. After lunch, I decided that we should give up on the house for the day and go for a swim in the pool.

I was in the water and Christopher was on the diving board about to jump in. We had been talking about automobiles and the lack of good mechanics in the area. Our conversation turned to car travel.

"It's really great fun," I said, "to drive down the pike at seventy miles an hour on a hot summer day with all the windows open."

"What did you say?" Christopher asked, starting to laugh.

"Why are you laughing?" I inquired.

"What the hell's a pike?" asked Christopher, obviously amused at my use of an antiquated word.

"Come on," I replied. "You ain't that young! If you really don't know, a pike is an abbreviation for turnpike, a highway!"

Suddenly it did sound a bit archaic, and I began laughing too. I don't recall using the word previously in relation to roadways and it is not in my working vocabulary. I usually use the term "highway."

That evening I thought that I would take Christopher, along with some other friends, to have dinner in the neighboring town of Woodstock, the artist colony famous for the rock festival, which in truth was held twenty-odd miles away. I chose to have dinner at Deanie's, a restaurant nationally famous for its relaxed atmosphere and excellent food. The menu had a card attached to it requesting that patrons inquire about the daily specialties of the house.

I called the waitress over to the table. "What's the specialty this evening?"

"Oh, some sort of baked whitefish. Pike, I think," she answered.

There was that word again—pike. It is not an unusual word, granted, but under the circumstances, not only odd but somewhat coincidental. Christopher and I looked at each other and began laughing again. The waitress and my other guests wondered what was so funny. "Inside joke," I told them.

We ate (I didn't have the pike), and ordered coffee and dessert. I excused myself from the table for a moment and went to the men's room upstairs on the second floor. Descending the stairway, on my way back to the table, my eye rested on a rather large painting hanging on a wall over the stairs. I looked in the lower right hand corner for the name of the artist and gasped aloud. The painting was signed, *J. Pike.*

When I got back to our table, I immediately told Christopher about the painting. This time we didn't laugh.

"'What do you suppose it means?" Christopher asked. I could see that he was becoming a bit uneasy over the persistence of the word.

"I don't know," I replied, "but I don't think it's coincidental. It's cropped up too many times. It might be some kind of symbol or omen with bearing and meaning on a psychic level. I'll meditate on it tonight and see what I get, what it means in relation to me or to you."

I am a believer that when omens or symbols appear, they are meant for the person to whom they are being presented and should be interpreted accordingly. I have been witness to many prophetic omens throughout my life and do not discard any lightly. If there indeed is a higher level of existence, then why wouldn't these entities from beyond attempt to give us warnings and guidance through passages presented symbolically, since they usually cannot contact our subconscious directly?

Upon my arrival home that night, I went into an immediate meditation and placed the word *pike* foremost in my mind. The only thing I received from a subconscious level was that the word related to a man, and that there was a heaviness, a sorrow connected with the word.

The following day was a Friday and at the local movie house *The Wild Bunch* was playing, a film that had stirred terrific controversy as to whether it was pro-violence or anti-violence. Since I am a movie buff and go as often as I can, I decided to see this controversial picture. Sam Peckenpah, the director, contended that he had attempted to create an anti-violence motion picture by literally filling the screen with as much violence as can be fit into one film, hoping to surfeit his audience with it until they would turn from violence. Most critics thought it accomplished the opposite and labeled it an extremely violent picture.

Midway through the film, one of the characters turned to the lead, played by William Holden, and addressed him by name. The character that Holden portrayed was named Pike. Another coincidence? A bit further into the film, another character referred to Holden by his complete name: Pike Bishop!

I was so numbed by this latest allusion to Pike that the rest of the movie held little interest for me. On the way home I really tried to tune into the symbolic Pike. I felt the violence of the movie I had just seen was somehow connected with the word. When I reached home I meditated and this time realized that all the omens related to *Bishop James Pike* and that there would be some violence, some tragedy in his life. I don't know why it took me so long to figure out what all those "pikes" meant, but when I finally did I didn't know what to do with the knowledge. Usually when a well-known person receives word from a psychic about impending disaster, it is taken as either a crackpot's dream, a threat by the one giving the prediction, or something to be ignored as not possibly having any significance or pertinence.

Often, when I have attempted to give prophetic information to someone, the outcome was not unlike the following scene from the beginning of *Julius Caesar*. When

Caesar and friends, followed by a great crowd, enter Rome in a glorious procession, a soothsayer calls to him from the throng:

SOOTHSAYER: Caesar!

CAESAR: Who calls?

CASCA: Bid every noise be still: peace yet again!

CAESAR: Who is it in the press that calls on me?
I hear a tongue, shriller than all the music
Cry "Caesar." Speak; Caesar is turn'd to hear.

SOOTHSAYER: Beware the ides of March.

CAESAR: What man is that?

BRUTUS: A soothsayer bids you to beware the ides of March.

CAESAR: Set him before me; let me see his face.

CASSIUS: Fellow, come from the throng; look upon Caesar.

CAESAR: What say'st thou to me now? Speak once again.

SOOTHSAYER: Beware the ides of March.

CAESAR: He is a dreamer; let us leave him: pass.

In this first meeting it is fascinating to note how quickly the negative prophecy affects Caesar. He dismisses the soothsayer with but one word: dreamer!

There is not one psychic that I have known or read about who has not at one time or another been labeled a dreamer. In my own life, I have been constantly accused of daydreaming. It wasn't until later in life that those who did accuse me thus came to realize that my daydreaming was directly connected with my psychic awareness, that I was reaching into my subconscious and seeing a reality that was not yet a part of the material world.

"He's dreaming again!" was a sentence I heard all during my childhood when I would attempt to tell my family of some prophetic feeling I had in regard to their future. I would constantly release myself into areas of the subconscious while in school, the often monotonous voices and teaching methods of my teachers affording fertile atmosphere for "drifting off." I have been rebuked for giving psychic advice in just the same manner that Caesar rebukes the soothsayer at their first meeting. "Cool it, Logan, you're a daydreamer!"

But in Julius Caesar's time prophecy was commonplace, something not to be taken lightly. Despite this, Caesar chooses to take no heed of the prophecy.

The negative portents and omens that are mentioned throughout *Julius Caesar* are ignored by Caesar. One of his servants tells Caesar that when the augurers sought prophetic advice by "plucking the entrails of an offering forth, they could not find a heart within the beast." Caesar misinterprets the omen as meaning that he would be a beast without a heart if he should stay at home and not go to the Senate. Even when the soothsayer again repeats his prophetic warning a few moments before Caesar is assassinated, Caesar brushes it off.

In our own day, there is evidence that several psychics gave fair warning to John F. Kennedy regarding any trips he might make to the South. These were brushed aside, with the prophet accused of daydreaming or being an alarmist who should be ignored and avoided at any cost.

It was with these very thoughts on my mind that I wondered what I should do with the symbolic omens that had come into my consciousness about Bishop James Pike. Our one connection was our publisher. I phoned Lee Barker, my editor at Doubleday, hoping I could reach the Bishop. Lee told me that Bishop Pike and his wife were off on a trip to Israel, attempting to track down the steps Jesus had taken during his ordeal in the desert.

Most of *The Wild Bunch* had taken place in the desert. Another coincidence? I knew that I had unconsciously aligned myself with Bishop Pike and that the psychic omens I had been made aware of were actually dire warnings for him. My unconscious ESP had been at work and in a very direct, unsubtle manner had shown me that Bishop Pike would meet with some kind of violence; possibly in a desert. "I feel he must be warned," I told my editor, trying to hide how frantic I felt.

"It might be difficult. He's most probably off on his own, but I'll see what can be done."

Frustration is sometimes the second name for one who knows something is going to happen but can do nothing about it.

A few days later, it was announced that Bishop Pike had been lost in the Judean desert. Some tribesmen had found his wife, delirious and wandering. Their vehicle had broken down and Pike had gone for help. That was the story Mrs. Pike gave reporters.

A week after Bishop Pike left to find help for his wife in the desert, his body was found. He had died from exposure.

I felt even more frustrated than ever. Couldn't I have received this symbolic information *before* Bishop Pike and his wife left for the Mideast? Psychics sometimes do develop guilt complexes in such cases. What eased the feeling of guilt was the impression that Bishop Pike had been on a suicidal mission into that desert. No one goes into an unknown desert without a guide, much less in an ill-equipped vehicle. Leaving his wife and going further into the desert says much regarding Pike's will to "join his son!"

It later dawned on me that no matter what the circumstances, Bishop Pike was to venture forth into that desert. There was no path for him to take but the one he did. I have been assured that he had been physically warned about going into the desert, and I believe him to have been a man who was so spiritually evolved that if he was not to have proceeded, he would have been afforded the information necessary to hold him back.

It was Bishop Pike's karma, as it was John F. Kennedy's and Julius Caesar's karma, to experience the kind of death they each did. No soothsayer, no psychic, no material change could have made a difference in the lives of these men in regard to the paths they would choose to travel.

The newspapers began calling me immediately. The story about my prediction concerning Bishop Pike's death first broke in the *Miami News,* September 8, 1969. I did not want to gloat over this successful prediction. It served no purpose for me to be concerned about what I felt to be a man's choice. I decided not to give any more interviews or answer any questions regarding it and I tried to put the entire experience out of my mind.

However, as I was in the midst of writing this chapter, the "Pike syndrome" started all over again. A neighborhood friend, Ruth Holumzer, asked if I would like to have some note paper she had gotten as a gift from her bank. The note paper reproduces a series of four watercolors depicting scenes of the lovely Catskill Mountain region in which we live. On the box cover was the label: "Heritage Savings Bank—Watercolors by John Pike."

The next day, while still writing this chapter, I picked up my copy of *TV Guide* (dated September 29, 1973) and opened it at random to page 91-A. At the very top of the page there was an advertisement for a TV premiere Movie of the Week. I read:

9:00 P.M.—Ch. 2 and 3—Western
       "The Wild Bunch"—Cast: Pike Bishop . . .
       William Holden, ...

A day or so later I had to take my car into New York City, and for some reason I took a different route than I usually do and found myself riding down the East River Drive. There was construction being done on this very archaic highway and it wasn't until I was miles away from where I wanted to get off that I was able to find an exit. I looked up at the street sign to discover where I was. The sign read: Pike Slip. I had never known that such a street existed in Manhattan.

I realize that several of these incidents might be regarded as coincidences or accidental (although I do believe in the Freudian theory that there are no accidents). It is even possible that I had developed some sort of psychic fixation with the word "pike" and unconsciously directed myself to where the word would appear. But I think that would be stretching believability a bit. There was too much unconscious direction that manifested itself in all too short a period of time.

I therefore believe that the word "pike" appearing as often as it did was an omen and that the feeling of dread I had initially received when placing this word in my meditation was symbolic of Bishop Pike's death. On an unconscious level, Bishop Pike was most probably reaching out, and my own psychic antennae were able to receive the messages from his being. The symbols had been presented to me and I had interpreted them correctly, but there was nothing I could do to prevent the event from occurring. The message was meaningful unto itself—Bishop Pike was to die in the manner in which he did, no matter what.

Over the years many people have written to me stating that they had become filled with a feeling of guilt after they had been made prophetically aware of an upcoming tragic event, did nothing about it, and then saw the prophecy come to pass. It is my contention that there was nothing that could have been done, that the situations were usually karmic in nature, and that the psychic information they had picked up, symbolically or otherwise, was either misplaced energies entering their aura or meant as a lesson for themselves.

There are symbols that appear to us consciously which signify prophetic events. In my own work, whenever I give a psychic reading I symbolically utilize color. The colors that I perceive in a person's aura have never failed to reveal something of that person's past, present, and future, and have much to do with what I have to offer in regard to his or her life.

I gradually discovered the meanings of the colors as I worked as a professional psychic. It wasn't anything that I studied (at least in this lifetime), nor for that matter was it anything I was even aware of. But, as people came to me for psychic advice, specific colors or color combinations repeated themselves in certain auras and I was able to devise the symbolic color meanings in regard to individuals. Although I have not been 100 percent correct in interpreting the various psychical manifestations which are utilized in my work, the color symbols have been extremely helpful, and uniformly they have been totally correct.

With regard to health, color in the aura means much to me. If I perceive the color blue or green around a person, I know he is in good health and will probably remain so, especially if the two colors combine to make a light blue-green.

The various shades of red, on the other hand, can signify a collapse of health. The brighter the color red in an aura, the more chance of an eventual health breakdown. If there is grey in an aura, I know that the person will soon be dead.

Purple usually means that the person is receiving healing, material or spiritual. The lighter shades of this color, especially lavender, generally connote that a person has a healing ability, whether he is aware of it or not.

These color symbols extend beyond the health area.

As the reading progresses, I find myself able to prophesy for the person based on the colors that emanate from his aura. They do change as the mood of the reading changes.

Red is always negative to me. And so is orange, a mixture of red and yellow, which I perceive as the light of a much confused person, one who is almost schizophrenic in nature, forever changing. Pure yellow, on the other hand, denotes a freedom of self, an achieved tranquility. Yellow is positive in nature and when dominant in an aura, means that an affirmative answer to a specific problem is in store.

I have never seen a brown aura in my symbolic color interpretations. I have no explanation for this. Of the times that I have seen black, I have had to sort out specific colors, for I perceive black to be a combination of all colors.

In aura reading, white is in the realms of the true masters and signifies that the person before me is going through his last incarnation on this plane of existence.

White or light gold signifies that the person is highly evolved, a soul that has been through many lifetimes and is spiritual to a vast degree.

The blues and greens when pertaining to spiritual evolvement tell me that the person is on the right path, that he is succeeding in overcoming personal karmic patterns from past lives.

Many parapsychologists believe that our senses present us with only the surface meaning of things. Everything we see, hear, taste, touch, and feel is merely an expression of some state of being which is objective to the consciousness it affects. This is a form of protection; for if we consciously psyched out the true, inner-depth history of all the objects that we come into contact with, we would be overcome by the mass of data and the states of being that actually lie beyond the familiar surfaces of everyday articles.

In other words, what we see in a material way is just *symbolic* of the real object in front of us. What a psychic does is to discern what lies beyond the surface of an object or a person, on a conscious level.

I have always been surprised at the number of people who are most successful in their first attempt at psychometry. The object that a person holds while attempting psychometry becomes the symbol of the real nature of the person or persons who owned it. While the symbolic object is being concentrated on, many truths relating to the owner of the object break through into the consciousness.

A letter arrived at my office on my birthday, April 24, 1974. It reads:

> "Dear Daniel Logan,
> I know you're very busy and do not expect any answer to this letter. However, after your visit to lecture and give a seminar for the Spiritual Frontiers Fellowship here in Rochester, I have been meaning to write you and have finally found the time.
> "When I psychometrized your ring at the seminar I got an impression of the person who gave it to you, as well as of the original owner. I didn't want to take up the group's time, since I knew that other people were waiting to volunteer. However, I saw that the person who gave you the ring was quite elderly, grey-haired, plump face somewhat lined, rather tending to have those brown 'liver spots' on her hands and neck. Frequently wears a single strand of pearls. The dress I saw her wearing was brown and white, with perhaps some grey; not sure of that.

At that seminar, I had decided to utilize the abilities of all those who came to the meeting, attempting to prove my point that we all can utilize innate psychic abilities which I feel every human being possesses.

I did not know the woman who wrote this letter and I am sure that she had no way of acquiring the psychic knowledge that she indeed did pass on to me. It was fascinating to me that she described the woman who gave me the cameo that made up the centerpiece of the ring. Several years prior to this, Louise Weller, a friend who helped me in my career, gave me this cameo; I haven't seen Louise for a number of years. Yet from touching the ring I had had made from the cameo (which happens to be a carved head of Mercury, messenger of the Gods), Ms. Diana Robinson of Pittsford, New York was able to pick up on the vibrations of Louise Weller of New Jersey, someone she had never met nor could have known anything about. Ms. Robinson could not have known if I had purchased the ring or if, in fact, it had been a gift.

Ms. Robinson had Louise Weller down to a tee, even to the string of pearls and a certain dress I recall Louise having worn to one of my lectures.

The letter continues to prove that not only past vibrations can be interpreted by the psychometrizer, but future, prophetic ones as well. At the time I had visited Rochester, I had just returned from an extensive promotional tour for another book. Ms. Robinson picked up this exhaustion, which I was trying carefully to hide, and the prophetic impression that I might become ill in the near future. To continue her letter:

> I was concerned for your health. I had the impression that you were driving yourself so hard that your motors were liable to blow apart in the near future.

The letter came some time after I had returned from Rochester and had indeed gotten very ill. The odd part of the letter was the wording. I had indeed felt that I might blow apart. There were times when my brain felt as though it would come right out the top of my head in some kind of explosion!

This illness was not publicized and Ms. Robinson, living hundreds of miles from me, could not have known anything about the brief period of near mental and physical collapse that hovered around me for a period of many weeks.

Psychometry, or object reading, is a most interesting form of sensing certain psychic symbolic vibrations of others. In any given group it usually has a great chance of success if deep concentration or a meditation is done beforehand.

In the Orient, the omens and symbols which appear in a person's experience are very carefully considered and taken quite seriously. Priests and others who delve into areas of the subconscious are sought out to interpret the meanings of symbols and omens. So much of what is perceived is symbolic that the Oriental actually lives on almost two completely different levels of experience: the physical, where things are what they seem; and the spiritual or subconscious, where certain objects and occurrences merely represent deeper aspects of what is materially evident.

The "inscrutable" Oriental is often working on this unconscious level. And it has been so deeply ingrained in him, has been made so much a part of his culture over the centuries, that despite modernization and the reflection of Western ways, the Oriental cannot help but approach his daily routine with this higher-leveled subconscious awareness.

While living in Japan, I was made aware of this double life which is lived by many Japanese—and which has led Western scientists to label the Japanese as the first schizophrenic nation in history.

The great and multi-talented Pulitzer Prize winning author, Yukio Mishima, committed suicide because he was unable to balance this innermost, innate spiritual awareness with his fantastic material success and modernization. Mishima's body and mind could not successfully contain on equal levels this seeing things for what they might be as opposed to accepting them for what they seem to be.

Ryuske Tokunaga, who acted as my guide and interpreter, is one such friend who has tried to throw off much of Japanese background in order to advance in a present-day society. But the ingrained spiritual meaning of things has reached him so often on the unconscious level that I am only now beginning to realize the constant battle that must go on in such aware people who attempt to deny or forget their spiritual backgrounds.

A recent experience involving Ryuske Tokunaga is quite apropos here. In 1973 Ryuske decided to carry on a family tradition and open a restaurant. Having become a permanent resident in America, Ryuske chose his favorite city, New York, in which to open his business. At that time, however, there seemed to be a plethora of Japanese restaurants in New York. Deciding on the best location was most important if the business was to be a success.

With the determination that is so overwhelmingly a part of him, Ryuske took to walking all the New York City streets, searching for the right place. Finally he narrowed the prospective areas down to two, one of which was on Second Avenue between 74th and 75th Streets.

He went back to this section on several occasions, attempting to feel out the neighborhood's vibrations. On one of these visits, Ryuske came upon an antique shop in whose window there hung a huge, bronze Japanese lantern. On closer inspection, he discovered that there was an engraved symbolic house mark on the lantern (the respected families of Japan have house marks that no other household can utilize, a kind of family crest, done in a simple Japanese calligraphic symbol). Ryuske was taken aback, as the house mark on the lantern was one he had considered using as the symbol and name of his restaurant.

He entered the antique shop and inquired about the lantern; the person inside the store did not know where it had come from.

"How much is it?" Ryuske inquired, desiring to purchase the beautiful object. He wanted it, whether he used the house mark for his restaurant or not. But the price was high, and because of the bills he knew he would have in order to open his restaurant, he decided not to buy it. In retrospect, Ryuske felt that the lantern with the specific house mark was an omen of sorts—a prophetic symbol substantiating his feeling that this was the right area in which to open his restaurant.

During this period, I had not seen Ryuske for some time, and did not know of his experience in the antique shop until long after the fact.

It was around Christmas time and I decided to send out cards. For several years I had been purchasing cards with a conservation theme, usually wildlife scenes. I was impelled to do something different this year. My own unconscious awareness afforded me the message that I was to go to the Metropolitan Museum of Art and purchase my Christmas cards there.

At the Museum, I decided not to buy boxes of cards, but rather choose ones that would fit individuals who were a part of my life experience. There were several cards that had Oriental themes and I started to pick over these for my Japanese friends. I was immediately attracted to one with a photograph of an elaborate Japanese lacquered box. The top of the box was carved and engraved with a detailed symbol.

This is for Ryuske, I thought instantly.

When I got the cards home I proceeded to sort them out and began the tiring process of addressing them. I picked up Ryuske's card and decided that I should probably send him something a bit more what I felt to be to his liking—possibly a scene depicting Japanese rural life, of which I had purchased several. However, I was unable to choose any other card but the one with the box on it. It's his, I kept thinking, although on a conscious level I felt he should have something else.

The card was sent, and after a few days I got a call from Ryuske. He was very excited and practically demanded to know why I had sent the card I did.

"I don't know," I could only reply, "I just felt that you should have it."

"Out of all the house marks in Japan, you have sent a card with the symbol that I have been thinking of using as my restaurant's name," Ryuske said. "I don't think that this is a coincidence."

He then told me about the lantern and said that he was going to purchase it as soon as possible, regardless of price.

"I feel that the lantern and your card were meant as symbols to me," Ryuske continued. "They were brought into my awareness by forces that desire me to open my business in the section I have been contemplating. It is not coincidence."

It was too late for him to purchase the lantern. It had already been sold, but this did not seem to bother Ryuske very much, as he felt that the message was in his *seeing* the lantern, not in *owning* it. Soon thereafter, Ryuske found a specific location in the area he had been guided to and began work on the restaurant, which was to be called "Tokubei."

The day after Christmas Ryuske telephoned me again. This time he was even more excited. Another friend had presented him with a gift—the very lantern that he had seen in the antique shop!

Tokubei is a most successful restaurant, and Ryuske feels that one reason is because he followed the prophetic advice given to him by the omens presented to his awareness via the reoccurring house mark symbols.

It was the eminent and brilliant psychic and author, Eileen Garrett, who came closest to understanding the nature of symbols in regard to their meaning. Ms. Garrett said that a symbol was a sign, in some form or movement, which represented states of being that stretched away from it in time and space. A symbol can therefore be termed an ideogram or a hieroglyph which reveals hidden subtleties of being.

These symbols can tell us things about past, present, and future occurrences. They can guide us, if the time is taken to interpret them on a prophetic level of awareness.

Direct symbols, such as those of the reoccurring house mark, are much simpler to comprehend because of their direct materialization. It is the subtle, unconscious type of awareness that can confuse us. There isn't a living soul who has not done something which seemed impulsive in nature yet which in retrospect turned out to be most prophetic.

An obvious example is the man who for no apparent reason decides to take a later plane than the one he is booked on, and subsequently learns that the first plane crashed; or the woman who arises one morning and against all reasonable thinking, immediately goes to her doctor's office, whereupon he discovers a lump in her breast which is successfully removed because she acted quickly; or the child who suggests to his school chum that they walk a different route than the one they usually take and finds a ten dollar bill in the street. The list of "why-did-I-do-that? and-am-I-ever-glad-I-did!" is an endless one.

Albert Layman, an acquaintance of mine, is an executive in a very important Wall Street organization. In 1973, being heavily invested in the stock market, Albert woke up one morning and called his broker at 7:30 A.M., before either of them had left for their respective offices.

After apologizing for calling at such an early hour, Albert insisted that the broker sell a certain stock.

"How much do you wish to sell?" the broker asked.

"All of it," Albert demanded, "and it should be sold today."

The broker argued that this was a good stock, that in recent weeks it had climbed to an all-time high. "Why do you want to sell the stock, anyway?" the perplexed man inquired. "I think you're being foolish. It's one of the most secure stocks you have."

"I really don't have a good reason. I just want it sold today."

The broker reluctantly sold off the stock that day, believing the sale to be a major mistake for his far too impulsive client.

Two days later the phone in Albert Layman's office rang. It was his broker. Startled, incredulous, the man told his client that the stock he had been forced to sell had plunged the following day to an all-time low. Since the company itself was about to go out of business, it looked as though there would be no chance of its being worth anything at all. "How did you know this would happen?" the truly amazed man asked. "No one in the market would have predicted this solid stock going the way it did."

"I can't give you any concrete reason. I just felt odd, negative about the stock that morning and decided to get rid of it. When I think of it now, it does seem rather impulsive—and suppose it had gone the other way?" Albert was puzzled himself at his behavior. "I simply followed my impulse. I guess it was luck that it turned out the way it did."

My mother lives on Long Island, about fifteen miles from Manhattan. One day in the summer of 1973, she was set to go on a short shopping trip via the IRT subway, which tunnels beneath the East River to New York

City. When she awoke that morning, an uneasiness came over her and unconsciously she became involved in several other home projects which kept her busy until it was too late to take the trip. She decided she could put it off until the following week.

On the day she was supposed to go into Manhattan, a section of the IRT subway tunnel collapsed onto a passing train, killing one person and severely injuring several others. Many people were trapped below ground for hours in temperatures that were recorded at over 115 degrees.

This happened at approximately the time my mother would have been returning home—she would probably have been on that train!

Recently, a young girl sat down to telephone a friend. By mistake she dialed the wrong number. After the fourth ring, the girl realized that it was a wrong number, but she didn't hang up. Finally, on the other end of the phone she heard the heavy breathing of an elderly lady who had managed to push her own phone off the hook and onto the floor from its place on the table.

"Help!" the old lady whispered into the phone. "Please help me! I can't breathe! I'm sick!"

The girl ran to a neighbor's house, leaving her own phone off the hook. She called the police, who were able to trace the call. Within the hour, a rescue squad was at the home of the elderly woman, who was actually in the midst of a serious heart attack. Quick action saved her life. A seemingly misdialed phone number afforded this woman many more years of life. Or was it a wrong number?

The plummeting stock, the subway accident, the old lady with the heart failure might appear to have no connection. There are those who will say that they were coincidences, lucky ones at that. But it is my contention that these incidents are indeed related, and are of the same nature, each involving what I would term "unconscious ESP."

I believe, along with many parapsychology investigators today, that some people exert unknown, unsuspected influences over their own lives by unconsciously utilizing an innate, although unrecognized, psychic energy.

From my early beginnings in the realms of the psychic, I have believed that all persons have ESP, that it is not some "gift of prophecy from God" given to certain special people and withheld from others. I have thus always been put off by the Jeanne Dixons of the world who profess some extraordinary link with God or Divine Mind. This is nonsense—everyone has ESP. All that is needed to release this psychic energy, latent though it may be, is belief in it, concentration on it, and the daily practice of its power.

The unconscious kind of ESP I am now talking about does quite often manifest itself in the person who claims no psychic ability, who even denies its existence. When Albert Layman sold his seemingly excellent stock, I asked him why he did it.

"I got out of bed one morning," Albert explained, "and began thinking about my stocks in general. I was shaving. I recall nicking myself and being upset over it. At that same instant, this particular stock came into my mind. I immediately had this negative feeling about it. At first I thought it was that I had cut my face, but this feeling of negation couldn't be shaken. I tried to reason with myself that it was the best stock I had at that time. It didn't work. I literally trembled when I thought of the stock in question. So I sold it."

The teenage girl claims that she never before dialed the wrong number. "I was watching TV earlier in the evening, about three hours before I decided to make a phone call to a friend," the young girl said. "I think it was the six o'clock news. Whatever it was, it was a downer—lots of violence and all that. As I sat staring at it, I got this very bad feeling about this certain friend of mine. I had this urge to call and check her out. I put off the feeling for quite some time, maybe several hours. Finally, at around ten o'clock I got up and phoned her. I didn't recognize the ring on my friend's phone [an odd thing to say] and anyway, someone over there usually answers after the second ring. I was about to hang up, but for some strange reason I couldn't. I was sure glad I didn't; the poor old lady might have died otherwise."

In some way the TV program the young lady was watching had served to trigger her unconscious mind; the violence in the program she was watching was some kind of unconscious symbol. The prophetic thought flashed across her mind to get to the phone, and she interpreted it as meaning that her friend was in trouble, when in actuality it was the old lady.

The initial prophetic flash occurred to her around 6:00 P.M. At least three hours had passed before she dialed the wrong number. If the elderly woman had been having the heart attack at 6:00 P.M., she would have been dead by the time the police arrived. In other words, the young girl was not experiencing telepathy with the old woman; she had prophetically picked up the vibrations of the upcoming situation long before it even began to take place. The old woman said that there had been no warning of the heart attack. "One minute I was fine, just getting myself some tea—the next instant I was doubled over in pain."

In the case of Albert Layman, the nick with his razor was the unconscious ESP symbol for him to get rid of his stock. When I asked him if he often cut himself while shaving, he said no.

"When you do cut yourself, do you usually have some kind of impression like that of your negative response with the stock?" I inquired.

"That was the first time," he replied. "And most interesting was the fact that I couldn't shake the feeling about it. As I looked into the mirror, the name of this stock kept repeating itself in definite negative ways. I just knew that I had to get rid of it. Don't ask me how, I just knew!"

I know of many unconscious ESP warnings that my mother has received. For years she was afraid to state her feelings, but because of my own work in the field of parapsychology, she now speaks up quite often about her unconscious ESP warnings. She does not attempt to get these impressions psychically; what she does seems impulsive and sometimes rather strange. But more often than not, when she acts upon these unconscious ESP flashes, she comes out ahead.

"Mom," I asked her, "can you remember why you didn't go into the city that day? What was it that you felt?"

"Well, I got up that morning and as I was dressing, I felt strange. I had a feeling that something was going to happen to me. I had a bad night's sleep and thought of putting off the trip, even though I did have several things I had to get. I decided to go, thinking I was foolish not to. After breakfast, I still had this uneasy feeling, so I decided to do some ironing first. Then I just kept finding things to do around the house. The feeling was so strong that I sat down and prayed for a few moments. I couldn't get rid of the feeling the whole day. That train could easily have been the one I would have taken on my return home if I had gone into the city, it was about the time I usually do come home."

This chapter I am writing came to me through just such an unconscious ESP flash. I was in Boston giving a lecture-seminar at Boston University in October 1973; I was staying at the home of Ann Valukis, a dear friend in Natick, Massachusetts, just outside of Boston. There were several problems I had been having with the structure of this book.

I was trying to meditate and get some glimmer of insight on what to write, having been blocked in ideas for more than a week. I turned on the TV in order to relax and watched a rather inane program, "The Brady Bunch." The leading character was serving breakfast, and one of the children was reading a newspaper at the breakfast table. I believe that the storyline of the show concerned whether he should read at the table or not.

It's in the newspaper, I suddenly thought. Those words just popped into my head. *What's* in the newspaper? was my next immediate thought. The only thing I could think of was something that pertained to the book. I got up from the sofa and went through every paper in the house. I found nothing. Disgruntled and more than a little frustrated, I turned off the set. "Those damn Bradys are really dumb!" I recall saying aloud.

After the lecture I remained in Boston, giving psychic consultations. Two days passed and I picked up a local paper from Ann's table and began to browse through it. I was struck by a headline about halfway down the page: *The Unexplained.* Reading on, I instantly had the entire concept of this chapter.

My unconscious ESP had been at work several days before when I got the first flash to look through the newspaper. It wasn't until a few days later that the unconscious thought was to mean anything concrete to me. The newspaper on the TV program was the ESP symbol that triggered the final outcome of my discovering the story days later.

The article I read gave several examples of the workings of unconscious ESP. One story was that of a man who was accidentally asked to appear in court as a witness in a case of robbery. When he arrived in court, the subpoenaed witness told the judge that he didn't know anything about the case. The police finally admitted that he had been called to the court by accident. The mistaken witness was about to leave the court when he hap-

pened to glance over at the defendant. To his amazement, he recognized the man as the one who had robbed
him of over a thousand dollars a few months before; the
case had never been solved.

When questioned, the man who had been called by
mistake said that he felt he had to go to court on the day
he did, even though his lawyer had told him that he could
most probably correct the mistake without appearing.

"Even though I had to take a day off from my job and
as against every feeling that I had regarding my appearance in court, I knew that I had to go. My wife was furious
with me, for she realized that my lawyer could have
straightened it out without me. I had no idea why I felt
so impelled to go—that is, until I saw the robber in court.
This is the strangest coincidence I've ever been
through!"

Again, I repeat what Sigmund Freud said: "There are
no accidents."

In countless ESP occurrences, the emotions play an
important part, as in the cases above. The train accident,
the dying old lady, the robbery—each of these would
involve highly emotional states of being for the persons
having the ESP occurrences. The prophetic aspect
comes into play when the ESP is triggered long before
the actual event takes place. If the newspaper which I felt
held the key to my problem with this book had actually
been in the house at the time I searched through the
papers, then this would be constituted as a merely tele-
pathic experience. But because the story was not published until days later, the experience can be labeled
prophetic. The emotion of frustration and complete anger with myself in not being able to formalize my
thoughts in my writing was the symbolic trigger.

Many professional psychics are highly emotional,
nervous people. Scientists are now working on the theory that this type of disposition and psychic awareness
are related in most cases. The emotions, when highly

charged, act as a trigger for the ESP. This can well explain why certain persons have a foreboding with no evident reason, later to discover that something had indeed happened to a loved one at the time of their discomfort.

However, ESP can be distorted by too much emotion as well as by too little. Professional psychics often find they score poorly on trivial questions ("What color earrings does my aunt wear?"), but also have trouble with queries of an especially emotion-tinged nature ("What should I do about my husband's cancer? Should he go to the doctor?"). A rough bell-curve graph helps to clarify this point.

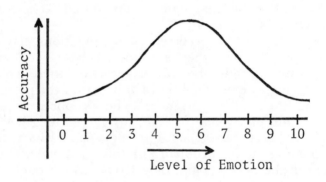

On the emotional scale, zero represents total apathy, while 10 might be an atmosphere of hand-wringing desperation. Highest prophetic accuracy seems to occur in the center, where the psychic and visitor are both interested in the answer, but neither is excessively concerned with the eventual outcome of the prophecy, wanting it to go one way or the other. This helps explain why most successful prophecies—and indeed, most instances of provable ESP—occur in a somewhat detached, "ordinary" state of mind that is neither indifferent nor desperate.

This easy-going state of mind is quite normal, of course, and so it's easy to see why unconscious ESP is able to operate in a wide variety of everyday situations. Dr. Rex Stanford is a parapsychologist at the University of Virginia who believes that a great deal of unconscious ESP occurs in many people's lives. He has documented case histories of persons who have been influenced by their unknown, unconscious extrasensory perception.

A young acquaintance of Dr. Stanford was one of six youths chosen to participate in the yearly Selective Service lottery in Washington on February 2, 1972. The young man reached into the lottery drum and withdrew a number which happened to be the birthdate of his own brother. The same number was simultaneously drawn by another person from a different drum. This meant, according to draft lottery rules, that the young man's brother would be exempt from the draft. The odds against this strange coincidence taking place are, to say the least, not only improbable but almost impossible.

Was it coincidence? Was it luck on the part of the young man's brother? Or was it the young man's unconscious ESP which led him to pick the lottery number that he did?

Let us consider the "good luck" theory. Unconscious ESP could well be the good fortune or luck that is attached to certain persons. How many times have you heard the following stated about someone you know?

"Good things always happen to him/her."

"He/she always seems to have good luck."

"Good fortune forever smiles on him/her."

"He/she is always at the right place at the right time."

Being at the correct place at the right time is the prophetic aspect of the good luck syndrome. When someone senses that the time is right (either to do something or *not* to do it) and the results are positive, then they have been using unconscious prophetic abilities. Persons who have continuous good luck are most probably utilizing their ESP quite often. Their powerful unknown or unrecognized prophetic abilities work for them in a constructive way, continuously bringing them into situations of a very positive nature.

But certainly practical *need* is also an important trigger for ESP, unconscious or otherwise. A friend of mine whom I'll call Matt is an editor at a large publishing house, but privately he's well known for his ESP ability. His secretary brought a friend of hers on impulse one evening, asking if Matt could give her a reading. Unfortunately, Matt had an appointment with someone, who was expected in about five minutes. So, though he had never seen the girl before, he quickly asked himself, "What does Mary *need* to know?"

"Have you checked your car radiator?" he asked.

She grinned wryly. "You're sort of right. I had to have the car fixed, and it's in the garage today."

"Well, you might check the radiator anyway," he mused. "Are you seeing a young man this weekend?"

"Yes and no. I'm going on vacation tomorrow, and I'll be seeing him before the weekend."

"I'm sorry, but I feel things won't go as pleasantly as you'd hoped. But if you make the best of it and bear up, everything should be all right."

Mary left, and Matt thought no more about it until the next morning, when he arrived at the office to find his secretary wildly excited. "Sit down!" she exclaimed. "You know what you told Mary yesterday?"

"Sort of," Matt mumbled, trying to remember.

"You said for her to check her car radiator. Well, when she got to the gas station, she found that whoever had drained the radiator hadn't put the drain on tight when it was refilled. It was half empty and would have boiled over on her way home. And her boyfriend—he's her fiancé really—she was going to see him today. But last night he called to say he'd been arrested for sleeping on the beach and possession of drugs, and he won't be able to raise bail until Friday."

Apparently Mary did make the best of it, because she and her fiancé are now happily married. In each case, Matt had picked up what was important to her—facts she needed to know *then*. Nor is this simply a matter of training: Matt always finds that he scores better when asked questions that really matter.

There are countless unconscious ESP experiences connected with artists, writers, and creative persons in general. Creative information is brought to them at the time of their desire to have it—and the process usually is completely unconscious.

Albert Bigelow Paine was the literary executor and biographer of the masterful writer, Samuel Clemens. In his *Mark Twain* (Volume III, Chapter CCLX) Paine relates the following example of unconscious ESP working for a creative person:

I am reminded of [an incident] of this period. Clemens was, one morning, dictating something about his *Christian Union* article concerning Mrs. Clemens's government of children, published in 1885. I had discovered no copy of it among the materials, and he was wishing very much that he could see one. Somewhat later, as he was walking down Fifth Avenue, the thought of this article and his desire for it suddenly entered his mind. Reaching the corner of Forty-second Street, he stopped a moment to let a jam of vehicles pass. As he did so a stranger crossed the street, noticed him, and . . . thrust some clippings into his hand.

" 'Mr. Clemens,' he said, 'you don't know me, but here is something you may wish to have. I have been saving them for more than twenty years, and this morning it occurred to me to send them to you. I was going to mail them from my office, but now I will give them to you,' and with a word or two he disappeared. The clippings were from the *Christian Union* of 1885, and among them the much-desired article. Clemens regarded it as a remarkable case of mental telepathy."

He told Paine that he had been drawn to walk down Fifth Avenue and that he had stopped for a long time at the Forty-second Street crossing, something he usually did not do. It was, I believe, his unconscious ESP that brought him into contact with the man who had psychically picked up Clemens's need to have the said clippings and had them in his hand the day he was to run into Clemens. This incident cannot be sloughed off as mere coincidence, nor a streak of luck for Clemens.

The man who gave the clippings to Clemens had the prophetic experience. After keeping the clippings for so many years, this man's unconscious ESP afforded him the reason for taking the clippings with him to mail to Clemens on the day he was to meet him. It was the right time.

It is important to note here that the nature of a person's state of being will make unconscious ESP work in either a negative or positive manner. Bad luck might also be attributed to unconscious ESP which works in the same, but negative way.

This phenomenon could well explain the "born loser," the constant failure, the accident-prone person. It is truly possible that in persons who think negatively, their unconscious extrasensory perception ability draws them to areas where accidents will occur, aligning the "unlucky person" with situations that will bring about the worst possible circumstances.

This is one reason why one should build up positive values when dealing with ESP. For without good vibrations around a person, the development of psychic abilities can be most destructive. "There are no accidents" —I do believe that Freud, who was most interested in psychic and occult matters in relation to his work in psychology, was trying to say that a negative person brings about the accident or unhappy occurrence unconsciously, through ESP, by placing himself in the path of the negative happening.

How else but through unconscious ESP does one explain the countless stories of persons who have saved themselves from hardships, tragedy, even death by impulsively acting on a feeling or a hunch at a particular time?

In the spring of 1974 my friend David Holumzer was watching TV with me. The program was interrupted by a news announcement that Patricia Hearst had been kidnapped.

"She's with them," David said in a very matter-of-fact tone of voice.

"What do you mean?" I asked.

"She's going to join them, she's with them," was his reply.

Now at that time, there was no evidence that Ms. Hearst was involved with the SLA in any way. She had been dragged screaming from her house, and her fiancé had been severely beaten by the kidnappers.

David's response was immediate and, as it turned out, was a correct prophecy. That Ms. Hearst had joined the SLA was not known or even hinted at by the press until weeks later. Something had triggered the prophetic statement in David.

I wonder how many other people got the same immediate impression. I would wager that there were quite a number. I am convinced that unconscious ESP symbols cross our paths every day, and if we were a bit more like the Orientals, we might be able to do much better as a nation.

Eventually, I feel that we will have "ESP banks," telephone lines, and other equipment for interpreting and utilizing the knowledge that we receive through these symbols that are brought into our lives on levels of awareness that have not yet been scientifically studied and documented.

Psychic energy has lain dormant for too many centuries, due to superstition, archaic religious beliefs, and a general fear of the unknown. Now is the time to utilize this energy for the most good that it can afford us. Unconscious ESP should be made *conscious* ESP, bringing this energy into daily use, making it work for us.

FOUR

Dreams Do Come True

One bright summer morning in the early nineteen sixties, Judith Bauer of Kingston, New York, got out of bed, came downstairs to her newly decorated kitchen, and proceeded to make breakfast for her family. Her husband and three children would soon follow.

Mrs. Bauer's concentration was poor that day, and she stumbled through breakfast preparations. The night before, she had dreamt far too vivid a dream. It had been especially disturbing since Mrs. Bauer recalled the dream in its entirety, something she had seldom done before. Mrs. Bauer had been interested in the occult and had read much in the field. She was somehow convinced that the dream was in some way a psychic one, and this upset her even more, for she couldn't make out what, if anything, the dream meant.

In the dream, Mrs. Bauer was in a place she had not been before. It was dark, possibly nighttime. The figures that appeared in the dream were clearly visible, but they were in a negative or X-ray form. Mrs. Bauer seemed to be a child, although her mind was quite adult. She was standing in the middle of a highway or a paved road of some kind which stretched ahead into a dark tunnel.

"I'm lost," Mrs. Bauer cried out in her dream. "Daddy, where are you? Help me, I'm lost."

Mrs. Bauer kept calling for her father, but there wasn't any response. Several persons walked past her on the sidewalk but none of them acknowledged her.

Then Mrs. Bauer heard her name being called. She turned completely around, and directly to her left was a long, very wide row of cement steps. At the top of the steps there stood a man who was calling her by her first name, Judy, and beckoning to her. He immediately started to descend the stairs, and as he did, massive stone columns—Greek or Roman, very ornate—rose up behind him. Upon reaching the bottom of the steps, the man walked toward Mrs. Bauer, hands outstretched.

As he drew close to her, she noticed that he seemed to be her father, both in stature, manner, and form of dress. But he had no face. It was a blank.

"Father," Mrs. Bauer addressed the man in the dream, "I'm lost. Can you help me?"

The man nodded but did not speak.

Mrs. Bauer took the man's hand, and as she did so, several other men appeared from behind some shrubs or short trees close by on the sidewalk. They leapt at the man and grabbed him away from her. One of the attackers threw the faceless man down on the sidewalk and began kicking him in the head.

The man who was kicking the fallen victim was very clearly represented in this dream: he wore casual clothes, slacks, a sweater over a white shirt, and sport shoes. The other men were all dressed in some sort of uniform. The man in the sweater bade the others join him in kicking his prey, and they proceeded to do so without any hesitation.

Mrs. Bauer recalled that the man in the sweater had on pointed shoes and was intent on kicking the back of the fallen man's head. Each time he did so, blood would gush out of a wound that had begun to form. The others were content with kicking any part of the body they could reach as the victim squirmed and tried to dodge the onslaught.

Suddenly, Mrs. Bauer saw that the fallen man's head had split. As the assailant continued his savage attack, the back of it began to give way and Mrs. Bauer awoke, drenched with perspiration and shaking from fear. The dream had been so realistic, so very forceful, that she had become sick to her stomach.

As she prepared the day's first meal, Mrs. Bauer decided that the dream, having been so vivid, must relate to her life in some way. She had to try to decipher its meaning.

Mrs. Bauer's father had died several years before, and she had not been that close to him. She couldn't understand why the man in the dream had come to her as her father in every way, albeit faceless. In fact everything about the dream was puzzling—the cement steps, the columns, the highway with the tunnel, the uniformed men led by the man in the sweater, and most confusing of all, the horrible assault on the fallen man.

Mrs. Bauer told her husband about the dream and he said to forget it: something she had eaten the night before or something she had seen on television must have given her this strange nightmare. However, it took several weeks for Mrs. Bauer to put the "nightmare" out of her mind.

Two months later the dream was repeated. It was exactly as the initial dream, only much more graphic in certain details. The men in the second dream had uni-

forms on, save once again, the man who did the kicking.
He was still dressed in sports clothes, sweater and all.
This time it was clear that there were stripes sewn onto
the man's sweater matching the stripes on the uniforms
of the other men. Moreover, the sweatered man now
appeared to have been beaten up himself; there were
marks on his face and one of his eyes was swollen and
blackened. The men in uniforms were also strange in
that they had no mouths. And as the top of the fallen
man's head began to give way, roses spewed forth with
the blood. It seemed a strange, ghastly sight. Mrs. Bauer
also heard a sound she had not been aware of in the first
dream. It seemed to be the sound of a large bird, very
loud, very clear, screeching as if in great pain.

This time the effects of the dream on Mrs. Bauer were
almost devastating. She became depressed and almost
stopped eating. Her every waking hour was spent in trying to figure out the dream symbols. She believed that
it had been no coincidence that the dream had occurred
twice, that something was trying to get through to her
on a psychic level.

For several days she did not tell her husband, not
wanting him to scoff as he had previously. But before
long Mr. Bauer realized that something was deeply trou-
bling his wife. When she finally consented to talk about
the dream, Mrs. Bauer couldn't contain herself and became quite hysterical.

The following day Mr. Bauer took his wife to see a
local psychiatrist. After three visits, the doctor dismissed
her, telling her he could find nothing mentally wrong
with her, that the dream was indeed baffling. He did feel
that most probably Mrs. Bauer felt hidden guilt about
her dead father, with whom she had never been close.
He offered no other explanation. Mrs. Bauer was given
a prescription for tranquilizers and told to take it easy
and get more rest.

Several more weeks passed. It was now fall and

Thanksgiving was approaching. Mrs. Bauer became even more anxious. She had an intuitive impression that something was going to happen during the holiday season. It was an impression that was somehow connected with her dream, and the anxiety that destroyed her peace of mind came from her inability to discover what the dream meant.

Mrs. Bauer began getting her house ready for a visit from relatives for the Thanksgiving holiday weekend. She was vacuuming the house with the TV turned on. As she began cleaning around the TV stand, Mrs. Bauer noticed that the afternoon game show she had tuned into earlier was no longer being broadcast. The buzz of the vacuum cleaner made it impossible for her to hear what the announcer was saying. His gestures seemed quite excited. Mrs. Bauer shut the vacuum off.

The date was November 22, 1963; President John F. Kennedy had been assassinated. Upon hearing the news, Mrs. Bauer again became hysterical and immediately phoned her husband at his office. He had already been informed of the killing and, as with millions of other Americans, his office was closing early that fatal day so that he could be with his family.

Mrs. Bauer's hysteria continued for several hours. Nothing her husband could say or do would bring her out of this state. Finally, she calmed down enough to be able to talk about her upset. At the instant Mrs. Bauer had heard the news of President Kennedy's assassination, she had understood the meaning of her dream, which was more than symbolic; it was almost a literal account of what had occurred on that fatal day.

The "father" in her dream was President Kennedy, who had been shot in the head—and a part of it had indeed come away, as it had in her dream. The man doing the kicking in the dream was Lee Harvey Oswald, one of the President's true assassins.

As the days passed and the tragic events unfolded,

Mrs. Bauer was able to match many of her dream details to the reality of the assassination.

Mrs. Bauer had often thought of President Kennedy in a fatherly manner. She had wished that her own father might have had the qualities and virtues that the President possessed. The cement steps and the massive columns in her dream were those of the White House and other buildings in Washington. The highway that she stood on in the dream was the one on which President Kennedy's autocade in Dallas would travel, the tunnel being the underpass just beyond. A second deeper interpretation of the dark tunnel ahead on the road is, quite naturally, death.

The blood is meaningful unto itself. The roses coming out of the President's head were the ones carried by Mrs. Kennedy and covered with her husband's blood.

Parts of the dream remained a mystery until later on. The men who helped in kicking the fallen father image might possibly symbolize psychic information that there had been more than one assassin. The fact that they were in uniform, Mrs. Bauer took to mean that possibly either the Army or the United States government itself had something to do with the murder, or that at least the murderers belonged to some sort of an organized group. Most importantly, the sweatered man did have stripes sewn onto his sports clothing. To Mrs. Bauer, this suggested that Oswald himself was in some way connected with this organized group—although Oswald was once in the Marine Corps. For years this aspect of her dream bothered Mrs. Bauer, who was a firm believer that the United States government would be above such misdeeds. In light of the Watergate scandal and all that ensued, Mrs. Bauer now feels that her dream can be taken quite literally.

The sweatered man appeared beaten up in the dream, eyes blackened, face swollen. Oswald appeared in just this manner after his arrest. The bird screeching in the background? Here are Mrs. Bauer's own words on this: "I do feel that the bird screeching was a large bird. I think, or rather believe, that it was an eagle, our country's symbol. I am convinced that the bird was crying because of the events which were taking place in the dream, and the outcome it would have on the country. In effect, the bird screeching represented sorrow for the country."

Mrs. Bauer has not had such a symbolic, meaningful dream before or since, and although the actual happenings took place within a short period of time, the events of the dream included elements of past, present, and future. The past was best represented by her father and herself as a child, and the future was suggested not only by the uniformed men—connoting the possibility of conspiracy—but by the grieving eagle.

Mrs. Bauer feels that had she been able to translate her dream earlier, she might have been able to communicate its meaning to the White House in some way, giving the President at least some warning. This, of course, does not mean that anything could have been done to make Kennedy any more cautious in regard to public appearances, for there are on record hundreds, if not thousands, of persons who had similar dreams, feelings, or just plain "hunches" about the late President being assassinated. Jeane Dixon's highly touted "black cloud over the White House while Kennedy is in office" was the most famous of the assassination predictions that came long before Kennedy himself ever even thought of going to Dallas.

Mrs. Bauer first related her dream to me via a letter she wrote several years ago. The details were given to me at length when I had a chance to meet her. She is a very unassuming person, completely direct and with no apparent need for any kind of recognition. In fact, as you might have guessed, the name Bauer is a pseudonym. The lady did not want her real name in print.

The dream is still devastating to Mrs. Bauer and I feel justifiably so. Why did she have the dream? What possible good could it have accomplished? She cannot answer these questions—the incident is still a major thorn in her side, something she has to live with. Thinking about it or speaking of it, Mrs. Bauer still carries the effect of the dream. Her peace of mind disappears and she wrings her hands constantly until talk of the dream ceases.

Why and how do any of us have precognitive dreams that come to us perhaps only once or twice in a lifetime, but are so exact when interpreted correctly?

Edgar Cayce*said: "Sleep is a shadow of that intermission of life or that state of death. The physical consciousness is unaware of existent conditions except for those senses which are on guard working through the auditory sense. This is more universal in aspect. The organs governed by the subconscious continue to work. The sense of perception related to the brain is asleep. The auditory sense, however, is subdivided and there is hearing by feeling, hearing through the sense of smell, the act of hearing through all the senses that are independent of the brain centers, but are rather of the lymph centers or the entire sympathetic system so that in sleep one is more aware even though the physical body is asleep. The sixth sense is a part of the superconscious, which is the spiritual self. . . . It is that which may be trained or submerged or left to its own initiative until it makes war with self, resulting in disease, temper, ..."

"This causes the brain to become so charged as to respond in the same manner as a string on a violin which is tuned to vibrate to certain sounds according to the

* The quotes in this chapter by Edgar Cayce are derived from his 1,009 dream readings interpretations, on file at the Association for Research and Enlightenment in Virginia Beach, Virginia. They are open to the public upon request. The number following each quote refers to the Reading quoted.

tension. The sense that governs this is in touch with the high self. There is ever, when the body is asleep, *that other self which communes with the soul of the body*. The sixth sense goes out at night to those realms of experience related to *all levels of consciousness, all time,* and to its own criterion or standards, developed through the ages. As a result . . . understanding may come. . . ." (5754–1)

And so it would seem in the case of Mrs. Bauer and her dream of the Kennedy assassination. Her sixth sense was at work during sleep and permitted her soul to search *another level of consciousness* where the imprint of the coming tragedy was evident. The actual events of November 23, 1963, did indeed involve her in some way. It is rare that a person does not dream of himself, or being somehow related to the situation that might occur in the dream.

"Extra Sensory Perception in dreams," Edgar Cayce stated, "is the activity or power of the other self. What other self? That which has been built by the soul's experiences as a whole, in the material as well as the cosmic world. Or it is a soul faculty of the soul body. Hence the subconscious is able to become aware of this activity when the body is asleep. When the physical consciousness is at rest, the other self communes with the soul body. It goes into those dimensions of consciousness where exist the records of all experiences and it judges persons accordingly." (140–10)

The old adage that the subconscious knows everything is most clearly seen here. Many of us strive to psychic awareness through meditation or other self-disciplines. But there are times, as in the Bauer-Kennedy dream, that the subconscious feeds us awareness during sleep; it comes without seeking.

Many dreams which later prove correct involve the death of a loved one or one who is much thought of— death creating the ultimate emotion in those left behind.

Dr. W.H. Tenhaeff of the Parapsychological Institute of the State University of Utrecht in Holland had a study made of the ESP elements in dreams. Some of the persons studied were asked to systematically record their dreams for over a year.

"This investigation," Dr. Tenhaeff was to write, "revealed that not only the recent past but also the near future was reflected in dreams. The statistical arrangement of the material obtained caused it to be seen that there was justification for declaring the prophetic dreams, later fulfilled, to be chance coincidences. An appreciable portion of the dream material produced proved to be connected with unexpected deaths, a specialized interest related to a psychic trauma."

There seems to be a definite association factor between precognitive dreams and deep emotional experiences. It is as though the mind, in sleep, hoping to escape the harsh realities of an emotional upset, reaches deeper into the subconscious where past and future experiences are stored. Emotion, then, becomes the floodgate of psychic experience in dreams. This can be borne out by the vast numbers of people who have precognitive dreams when they have had or are going through an emotional crisis in their lives.

Once again, I discovered Shakespeare had much to say about predictive dreams, especially at a time of deep emotional crisis.

"I dreamt my lady came and found me dead" are the words spoken by Romeo in Shakespeare's great tragic romance of young love. The young Romeo has gone through several major emotional experiences—love, death of a close friend, murder—and he has had this precognitive dream. Ironically, the words are not spoken out of fear or any other negative emotion. Romeo says them in the middle of a quite joyful speech. Romeo states that the dream he has had was strange and wondrous because in it his lady Juliet . . .

. . . breath'd such life with kisses in my lips,
That I reviv'd, and was an emperor.
Ah me! how sweet is love itself possess'd,
When but love's shadows are so rich in joy!

Had the youth been able to interpret the dream correctly, he might have realized that his dream was a kind of reverse symbolism—something which sometimes does occur in fact. What actually does happen in Act V is that Romeo drinks the poison from the apothecary and says, "Thus with a kiss I *die*,"as he kisses what he believes to be the lifeless form of Juliet. Furthermore, when Juliet awakens in the tomb, she discovers Romeo's body and attempts to kiss the poison from his lips—yet another reversal of Romeo's dream, in which she breathed life into his lips instead of extracting death from them. Romeo's dream, then, takes on new meaning, at least to us.

Let me state here that it is completely legitimate to interpret the dreams of characters found in Shakespeare and in other works of writing. The results Sigmund Freud made of a study into dreams that occur in literature was published in 1907 under the title, *Delusion and Dreams in Wilhelm Jensen's "Gradiva."*

Freud became interested in the subject in 1906 when Carl Jung questioned him as to the probability of analyzing invented dreams. It seems that Jung was reading a novel in which the leading characters were having dreams which in many ways related directly to their personalities. Could the dreams that appear in literature, those that are artistically constructed, indeed be analyzed? Freud decided he would attempt to answer the question.

Freud proved beyond a doubt that fictional dreams and nightmares did function as real ones. In his *Autobiographical Study* (1925), he again put forth the theory that artificial dreams could be interpreted in the exact same way that real dreams are. He also made it very clear that "this new-found insight was one of the original paths from my understanding of the dreamwork to my analysis of artistic creativity and imaginative writing."

In other words, dreams recounted in great literature are one of the main connections Freud discovered between dreaming and the creative imagination in general.

Romeo's dream has all the properties of a real-life dream: it is deeply prophetic and has elements of wish fulfillment. In becoming an "emperor," Romeo feels that he will be able to have power over both his own and Juliet's father (who has tried to stop their love affair) and also the Prince who has banished him. He did not once feel that this revival as an emperor might have meant awakening in heaven.

More amazing is the fact that the dream occurs in Shakespeare's most formal, most stylized, and in many ways, his most artificial play. Thus, Romeo's dream remains a paradox of literary realism: It is a completely realistic event which exists in a very formal, completely unreal atmosphere.

Many critics through the ages have called *Romeo and Juliet* Shakespeare's "dream" play. The entire play has a dreamlike effect; the young romance is treated almost as a dream, including the balcony scene. In fact, Romeo says these very words during the balcony scene:

> *O blessed, blessed night! I am afeard*
> *Being in night, all this is but a dream,*
> *Too flattering-sweet to be substantial.*

And at the most spiritual level, Romeo's dream turns his forthcoming death into being newly born. Freud said that this was a dream that at every level explains to us the ability of dreams to prophesy in reverse.

One of the most annoying aspects of psychic dreams is not knowing whether the dream is to be taken as presented or to be interpreted in reverse. In many instances, unfortunately, only time can answer. I do believe that if the occurrences in a dream are quite out of the

ordinary, very farfetched, or as in Romeo's case, ro-
manticized, then one should be wary of a reverse happening.

In Shakespeare's *Julius Caesar* the interpretation of
dreams also plays a most important role. The first dream
mentioned in this drama is one dreamt by Calpurnia, the
wife of Caesar. It is Caesar who relates the dream:

> *Nor heaven nor earth have been at peace tonight.*
> *Thrice hath Calpurnia in her sleep cried out*
> *"Help, ho! They murder Caesar!"*

Decius Brutus is intent on getting Caesar to the Senate
so that the bloody deed can be accomplished, but Caesar
explains further:

> *Calpurnia here, my wife, stays me at home.*
> *She dreamt tonight she saw my statue,*
> *Which, like a fountain with an hundred spouts,*
> *Did run pure blood, and many lusty Romans*
> *Came smiling and did bathe their hands in it.*
> *And these does she apply for warnings and portents*
> *And evils imminent; and on her knee*
> *Hath begged that I will stay at home today.*

Decius Brutus, catching the moment, purposefully
gives a misinterpretation of Calpurnia's dream to Caesar:

> *This dream is all amiss interpreted;*
> *It was a vision fair and fortunate.*
> *Your statue spouting blood in many pipes,*
> *In which so many smiling Romans bathed,*
> *Signifies that from you great Rome shall suck*
> *Reviving blood, and that great men shall press*
> *For tinctures, stains, relics, and cognizance.*

The fantastically egomaniacal Caesar accepts this
wrong interpretation of the dream and goes to his death.
This dream should have been interpreted literally.

Caesar was aware of the political situation making the dream's probability not that farfetched. He should have been forewarned.

It is a historical fact that Calpurnia had this prophetic dream of Caesar's death; reference to it can be found in *Parallel Lives* by Plutarch, the eminent Greek essayist, historian, and biographer. Shakespeare was to discover much material for his own works by absorbing the writings of Plutarch.

Calpurnia's dream is not the only prophetic one in *Julius Caesar.* Marcus Brutus dreams that he will die at Philippi, which he later does.

The subconscious part of our mind does often dream accurately, but the dream is sometimes filtered by the conscious mind, giving the dreamer a kind of protection from the truth. If we escape truth in real life on occasion, why then can we not sometimes escape it in dream states as well?

Another precognitive dream that concerned death is the often quoted one of Abraham Lincoln's. This was not a dream in reverse prophecy, rather one that foretold in great detail the actual events that would follow. Quoted below are the exact words spoken by President Lincoln long before the assassination:*

> There seemed to be a deathlike stillness about me in the dream. . . . I heard subdued sobs, as if a number of people were weeping. I thought I left my bed and wandered downstairs. There, the silence was broken by the same pitiful sobbing but the mourners were invisible. I went from room to room; no living person was inside, but the same mournful sounds of distress met me as I passed along. I was puzzled and alarmed. What could be the meaning of all this?
> I arrived at the East Room which I entered.

* Quoted by Jan Ehrenfeld in "Telepathy and Medical Psychology."

There was a sickening surprise. Before me was a
catafalque on which rested a corpse in funeral vest-
ments. Around it were stationed soldiers who were
acting as guards; and there was a throng of people,
some gazing mournfully upon the corpse, whose
face was covered, others weeping pitifully. "Who is
dead in the White House?" the dreamer asks.

"The President" someone replies. "He was killed
by an assassin." I slept no more that night and was
strangely annoyed by the dream ever since.

Many persons who have been the victims of assassins,
or who have lived during the time of assassination
attempts, have dreamt of the actual events which would
take place at a later time. One such account involved the
assassination of England's Spencer Perceval, who was
the Prime Minister and Chancellor of the Exchequer. He
was shot in the lobby of the House of Commons on May
11, 1812. Dr. John Abercrombie had this dream experience related to him before the actual event. The following excerpt is from Dr. Abercrombie's book, *Inquiries
Concerning the Intellectual Powers* (1838):

The dream came to John Williams who resided in
Cornwall eight days before the actual assassination
was committed. Mr. Williams dreamt that he was in
the lobby of the House of Commons, and saw a
small man enter dressed in a blue coat and white
waistcoat. Immediately after, he saw a man dressed
in a brown coat with yellow basket buttons draw a
pistol from under his coat, and discharge it at the
former man, who instantly fell—the blood issuing
from a wound a little below the left breast. Mr. Williams saw the murderer seized by some gentlemen
who were present, and observed his countenance;
and on asking who the gentleman was who had
been shot, he was told it was the Chancellor. He
then awoke and mentioned the dream to his wife
who made light of it—but in the course of the night

the dream occurred three times without the least
variation in any of the circumstances. He was now
so much impressed by it, that he felt much inclina-
tion to give notice to Mr. Perceval, but was dis-
suaded by some friends whom he consulted, who
assured him he would only get himself treated as a
fanatic.

On the evening of the eighth day after, he received the account of the murder. Being in London
a short time later, he found in a news shop several
colored prints depicting the scene, and recognized
in it the countenance and dress of the parties, the
blood on Mr. Perceval's waistcoat, and the peculiar
yellow basket buttons on Bellingham's (the murderer's) coat, precisely as he had seen them in his
dream.

An interesting note here is that many dream
interpreters have stated that the dream wasn't of Perceval's actual death, but rather of the colored prints that
the dreamer was later to find in the news shop. Many
people dream of stories, pictures, and headlines which
will later appear in the newspaper or on television. Not
only does the news-shop theory make painful truth more
acceptable, it also reinforces the theory that a dreamer
picks up what relates directly to him.

Elsie Sechrist, whom I mentioned earlier, is one of the
foremost authorities on dreams in the world. She explains that there are four kinds of dreams: the physical,
the mental, the emotional, and the spiritual. There are
also four sources of these types of dreams. First there
is our own subconscious with its various levels. Then,
there are the times when we are able to communicate
with the subconscious of another. Third is the superconscious. Fourth is God (the world of the soul or Spirit).

Physical dreams, as Edgar Cayce also stated, are
created by the senses that are not silenced by sleep.
These occur in the upper level of the subconscious,

created by feelings, sounds, smells, and other senses that continue around the sleeping person. Usually we do not respond to the senses being utilized unless they are truly attacked—as by loud noises, extreme changes in temperature, movement, and so forth.

On the physical level, we dream about things that have occurred during the hours we are awake. On this level we have what are known as wish-fulfillment dreams.

From the deeper level of sleep we reach into the realms of the mental and emotional—dreams that involve our friends, business associates, and people we do not know. Symbols which depict the emotional and mental stresses of our mind come through on this level of the dream state, usually in the form of arguments, fights, attack by wild animals, and all other forms of violence. Psychiatrists agree that these dreams are usually warnings of mental problems and deep emotional disturbances which are about to get out of hand.

Precognition, telepathy, clairvoyance, spiritual awareness, and all forms of prophecy come to us in the dream state when we reach the superconscious area of the mind. Creative and inspirational dreams occur when one reaches the superconscious level of dreaming.

The psychic, superconscious area of the mind has been utilized through the dream state by a great number of successful persons. George Frederick Handel, for example, received the melody of the last movement of *The Messiah* while dreaming. Many of Benjamin Franklin's inventions were first presented to him while he was dreaming.

The Singer sewing machine, with its innovative ideas, was first dreamed by its inventor, who was having much difficulty with it during his waking hours. Singer could not discover how to make the needle on his invention and had been attempting to develop a needle with a hole at the base. This never quite worked out. The answer to his problem came to him in symbolic form during a dream. Singer dreamed of many knights in armor who were carrying extremely sharp lances. The knights were mounted on fine steeds and the lances they held were resting on stirrups. At the point of each lance there was a hole. Remembering the dream upon awakening, Singer jotted it down. He recalled that the holes were at the *tips* of the lances and realized that the needle on his machine had to have the hole at the tip instead of at its base, as he previously thought. His dream changed an entire industry.

Countless writers have dreamed their stories before writing them. Robert Louis Stevenson received a complete outline for his great *Dr. Jekyll and Mr. Hyde* while he was in a dream state. This again reinforces the associations Freud made of creativity and the imagination during dream states of consciousness.

For a dream to be truly prophetic, however, it must qualify in several respects. If a man dreams that his father will soon die and the father does indeed pass away, we must take into consideration the facts at hand. Was the father ill before the dream took place? Did the son know of the illness? Or, did the son dream of his father's demise without any prior knowledge or awareness of poor health?

If the person dreamt of his father's passing without any foreknowledge of the man's being ill, then the dream was indeed prophetic.

But there are still other explanations for seemingly prophetic dreams that in truth are not, and these should be considered before anyone decides that his dreams foretell the future. In many cases, people are determined to make their dreams come true, and either consciously or unconsciously, they make choices in the waking state that will compel their dreams to become a reality. (This is the so-called "self-fulfilling prophecy.") In other instances, persons so desire their dreams to come true that they tend to forget the original dream, elaborating on it and garnishing it with prophetic frills *after* the fact!

It was the wise Oriental who said that we live in a world of ten thousand things, and that at one time or another we dream of these ten thousand things. Persons will sometimes dream of certain combinations of things and occurrences that they will later find happening in their waking lives.

A person dreams of a large house with a porch and a white door. In the dream it is raining. Months, maybe years, pass, and in that time the person has undoubtedly come across the entranceway of many houses. On one particular day he comes to a house that has a white door and a porch. It is raining. Immediately, the person believes that he had a precognitive dream experience. This is a possibility, but more probably it was just coincidence, a chance happening. Sooner or later, the law of averages will make some dream out of the thousands we have seem to be prophetic in nature.

We are constantly being bombarded with images in the media. We see photos, films, broadcasts of places we have never visited, and these images are registered on our subconsious mind. Years later, after we have forgotten these images, we can utilize them in dream states of consciousness. Then, if we happen to get to these places, we can rightly feel that we have dreamt of them before— but not necessarily in a prophetic way.

Scientists have used the above explanations to debunk supposed prophetic dreams whenever possible. But in many instances there can be no reasonable explanation other than that certain dreams are indeed precognitive.

Over the years, I have had letters written to me by people who profess to have had prophetic experiences. In most of these instances the prophecy came to the person while he or she was in a dream state of consciousness. And, in almost all of these cases, the person reports that the prophetic dream he or she has had is a rare occurrence, something that is not usual. (Again, this supports my contention that we are all psychic to a degree, and that we all have psychic experiences at one time or another in our lives.)

A recent letter from a lady in Lancaster, Pennsylvania, is but one example:

> Although I lead a most normal life and do not consider myself to have ESP in any way, I have had a few dreams in my life that have been frighteningly accurate. One particular prophetic dream, which I had twice, involved my second child, a son. I had just discovered that I was pregnant with him. That very night I had a dream, more like a nightmare, of what would occur to him at birth. In the dream he was gasping for air and began to turn blue. His heart "appeared" to be very slow and he "felt" cold, lifeless. I saw the doctors working on him. Finally, he was placed in a box of sorts. I couldn't get to him.
>
> Upon awakening I was in a cold sweat and most upset. I reasoned this off as a bad dream. Two days later, I dreamt the same thing. After many consultations with my doctors, who convinced me that this birth should be as smooth as my first one had been, that I had no health or mental problems, I decided that in truth I did have what amounted to be silly dreams.
>
> Complications with this pregnancy did arise, however, and my son was born in seven months instead of nine. The birth was exactly as I had dreamed . . . there was much gasping for air and the baby turned blue. There was hardly any heartbeat and I was told that he was ice cold. The box they placed him in, after working on him for an hour, was an incubator.
>
> I do not know why I had this dream, which proved to be correct in every detail. I can even recall what some of the doctors and nurses looked like in the dream. There wasn't any physical way for

me to be aware of what would occur at my son's birth, seven months beforehand. There is no history of premature births in my family or my husband's. I am a positive person, not taken to gross dire imaginings. I have had three more children and did not have one fleeting moment of anxiety over their births. I do not know why I had this dream that foretold the exact circumstances of my son's birth.

I am wondering if I had taken the dreams seriously, would I have not been able to have had a more easy time with it. As it was, I was visiting my parents, hundreds of miles away from my own home when the initial labor pangs began. I was in no way physically or mentally ready for an early birth. But, had I taken this dream as prophetic. . . .

Inasmuch as this woman had no external reasons for her dreams, it is indeed a precognitive one. And, as is the case with many such dreams, had she approached it as a warning, she might have avoided some of the complications which ensued. Precognitive dreams can be of value to those who have them.

A childhood friend of mine in which she had a series of dreams envisioned herself talking to thousands of persons who were gathered in huge halls. She appeared most happy at the start of the dream, but as time went on she became tired and began to cry in front of those people in the audience.

Years passed and my friend decided to have a career in films and made several. At first she was most happy with the glamorous life she was leading, but soon she became bored with the roles she was forced to play and the business aspects of a film career. She proceeded to have crying spells, and after a time she married and abandoned her career. The dreams this woman had were indeed prophetic.

Two things are interesting to note here: Prophetic dreams sometimes come in series, occurring more than once. And, as stated before, prophetic dreams are related to the strong emotions of fear, sadness, rage, and so forth. Countless numbers of people dreamed that the *Titanic* would sink long before it did. The *Hindenburg* disaster, the assassination of the Kennedy's, and other occurrences which conjured up deep emotions in the minds of many were all recorded as dreams long before the actual events.

Only in recent years has science seriously begun to investigate the nature of prophetic dreams and how they can be applied to our waking state. The July 3, 1967, issue of *The Journal of the American Medical Association* tells the story of the disaster which occurred in the Welsh village of Aberfan. In the early morning hours of October 21, 1966, a coal slag slid down a mountain on top of this village, killing 144 persons, mostly children.

Dr. J.C. Barker of England investigated to see if anyone might have prophetically felt in some way that the tragedy would take place. Almost sixty British men and women reported that they had feelings of the disaster days or even weeks before it happened. Forty-two of these accounts have been verified as prophecies because they had been reported to others long before the actual slide. At least thirty persons had dreams of the disaster happening exactly as it did.

Had the above dreams been recorded and taken seriously, very possibly the area of the occurrence might have been pinpointed and the town evacuated long before the fact. Many of the persons who had dreamt of the disaster had more than one dream, and in each of the succeeding dreams more evidential material was gleaned as to time, place, and surrounding events.

I do believe that the dreamer is the best interpreter of his own dreams. The symbols that are seen in a dream state of consciousness mean something entirely different to the person having the dream than to anyone he might relate it to—and that includes psychiatrists. The individual who is interested in discovering what his dreams might mean—especially in a prophetic way—should set up a procedure something like the following:

Write down your dreams as soon as possible upon awakening; often they are lost if anything else is brought to mind. You should keep pencil and paper near the bed for this purpose. If you make the suggestion to yourself just before going to sleep that you *will* remember your dreams, most probably you will recall them. Put this thought into your mind several times before drifting off.

You may awaken during the night with just a quick remembrance of the dream you've had. Write down whatever it is you recall, no matter how incidental it might seem; when you get up the next morning and check over your notes, you will usually be able to remember the entire dream.

The important things to remember in a dream are the setting, any people that appear, the colors, and any action or words.

Working on your dreams almost every day over a long period of time will bring much success. If the dream seems strange, you might be recalling only bits and pieces of it. There are times when mental blocks will erase your recall of dreams.

One thing that might be helpful in deciphering a dream is to suggest to yourself before going to sleep the next night, that the dream will be repeated. It usually is, and with extra details not recalled before.

Certainly dreams should not be treated in a light, offhand manner, as many people do. Dreams are meant as guidelines and can offer prophetic information when deciphered correctly. Errors are pointed out and confirmation of positive directions can be gleaned from psychic dreams. The work that is only now beginning in dream laboratories, such as the one at Maimonides

Medical Center in Brooklyn, New York, signals the
dawning of a new awareness in the realms of mind consciousness and expansion.

J.B. Priestley, one of the great minds of this century,
has shown a marked interest in the elements of time and
in his later works has written about time in regard to
prophetic dreams. Priestley has had two particular
dreams that bear investigation, for they convinced him
that prophecy in dreams is more than telepathy or ESP.

The first recognitive dream that Priestley had was
when he was a young man. In this dream he saw the
angry face of an uncle glaring at him. The face seemed
to be appearing out of a vague darkness. In waking states
of consciousness he had seen very little of this particular
uncle, and this was the only dream he had ever had of
the man. The light, steel-gray-blue eyes of his uncle were
most prominent in the dream and Priestley was terrified
of them. He had never seen his uncle express anger in
real life and had never even associated him with a bad
temper. But in the dream the man's stare was a half-mad,
enraged glare, though he neither spoke nor moved.
Priestley could not put this image out of his mind for
days. It haunted him.

Many years passed. Priestley, now a soldier in the First
World War, was home on leave. He was attending a
music hall show and was in the bar section of the theater
waiting for the second act to begin. Suddenly he had the
impression that someone was staring at him. Looking
down the dimly lit bar he spotted the uncle that he had
so long ago dreamed about. He was glaring at Priestley
in the exact same manner that he had done in that dream.
The same expression of rage reaching out from a half-lit
void almost threw the grown Priestley into a state of
complete terror. He went over to his uncle, who, as it
turned out, was angry at him for some past occurrence
that was not even Priestley's doing.

Later, Priestley tried to reason out the circumstances

at hand. Was it a coincidence that he had dreamed this happening many years earlier? It is not too surprising that a child should have a dream about some older relative staring at him out of the darkness. Most children express some unexplained fear about certain relatives, he argued with himself. It is also not too surprising that he should have met an angry uncle in the bar of a theater. It was not even too much of a coincidence that the relative was acting in the same exact manner as he did in the dream.

However, because he had an open as well as a brilliant mind, Priestley didn't just explain away his dream as some chance happening, some unrelated coincidence. He had never had a dream about a relative before, he reasoned, much less of one glaring at him out of the darkness. Also, at no other time did he ever encounter an angry uncle, or any other relative for that matter, in a bar or any other public place. The odds against both these things occurring—along with his uncle's identical half-mad expression—seemed to Priestley to be quite heavy.

J.B. Priestley had a second prophetic dream in the mid-1920's. In this dream he found himself in the front row of the balcony of a theater that was colossal in size, albeit vague in description. He was sitting behind a railing watching what he thought to be a stage, which was equally massive. On this stage, which had no definite proscenium arch, there was set before him the most brilliantly colored spectacle. Nothing moved, but everything was a mass of motionless, awe-inspiring color.

The dream stayed in Priestley's waking thoughts for months. He did not know just what he had dreamed, but it nonetheless was the most beautiful thing he had yet envisioned, either in a dream or a waking state of consciousness.

More than ten years later, on a visit to the United States, Priestley traveled across the country to see some of the sights. One morning he arrived at the site of the Grand Canyon. There was a heavy mist and, as is usually the case on unclear mornings at the Canyon, nothing could be seen of it. He took a seat on a rock close to the edge of the Canyon directly in front of his hotel and waited for the mist to lift. It disappeared most suddenly and Priestley was beside himself. Here was the brilliantly colorful, motionless and magnificent spectacle that he had seen in his dream! His recognition of it was instanta-neous—this was exactly the image that had appeared in his dream and haunted him years before.

Again, Priestley set out to debunk the theory that he might have had a precognitive dream. The Canyon dream had occurred long before he had an interest in time or precognition. When the Canyon had appeared out of the mist, there was instant, immediate, definite recognition. As in the previous case, there was again the long interval of time between the dream and the actual event. There were no strongly felt emotions in regard to these dreams, nor suppressed anxieties. There was no psychological explanation for Priestley's having had ei-ther of the dreams.

In both cases, Priestley has stated that he in no way could have manipulated his waking life, even on an un-conscious level, to bring those dreams to fruition. He did not know that the Grand Canyon was what he had seen in his dream until he had actually seen it. Some of his friends and aquaintances argued with him the possibility that he had seen and forgotten photographs of the Grand Canyon, but Priestley could not accept their argu-ment. When he had the dream, color photography was not yet in evidence, and color is the most important aspect of both the Canyon and the dream. And he further states that if he had seen a painting of it he surely would have recalled it, he certainly would have connected his dream with it. Both the dream and the actual event of seeing the Canyon had tremendous impact on him. His feelings on seeing the Grand Canyon both in dream form and in actuality, Priestley said, were the same—"there was a shared richness, a complete depth, an intricacy and a complete overpowering state of grandeur and magnificence which would make any comparison with vague memories of an old photo or painting seem utterly ridiculous."

Priestley also realized that he was not in the habit of dreaming about sitting in huge, strange theaters viewing a multi-colored, brilliant, never-ending spectacle. He always felt that in the dream he was in the front row of the theater, and when he caught his first glimpse of the Canyon, he indeed was sitting close to a railing, as he might have been in an actual theater. It was a circumstance he would not very easily have anticipated. He had never thought of going to America before he did and had no interest in seeing the Grand Canyon when he arrived. He was traveling by railroad from New York to the West Coast, and the opportunity to stop over at the Grand Canyon was a result of last-minute plans made while he was more than halfway across the country.

The Grand Canyon proved to offer a terrific fascination to Priestley and he visited it many times afterwards, even traveling to the bottom of it. The Canyon became the basis of his book *Midnight on the Desert*. It is his opinion that the precognitive dream was presented to him as a guideline, something that would instigate his investigation of the Canyon.

Priestley has denounced coincidence in regard to his two dreams because he believes that when too many details of a dream and an event agree, when the odds against chance are too great, and when the entire sense-feeling of a prophetic dream and the real event are completely out of the ordinary with chance encounters, then coincidence must be ruled out. It is at these times when coincidence turns into something quite different. Anyone who says that Priestley's prophetic dream experi-

ences were coincidences did not "see" the face of the
relative as he did, and did not "see" the fantastic color-
spectacle which was to be the Grand Canyon in a future
experience.

Priestley also believes that in precognitive dreams we
are dealing with something that is most difficult to study
under scientific methods, simply because the range of
dream experience cannot be brought under "control"
and therefore cannot be honestly "tested." I completely
agree. This is the single reason why I refuse to be tested
for my psychic ability: I feel it is a waste of the time and
ability I have been allotted in this life; I would much
rather be of assistance to the individual. Psychic phenomena, including prophetic dreams, have a way of with-
ering up and disappearing when scientific methods are
employed.

Priestley's comment on psychic investigators is most
apropos here: "It does not surprise me that experimen-
tal psychologists—some of them attempting to deal with
the psyche and psychic as if it were a lump of sodium—do
not have precognitive dreams: their minds are already
made up against them!"

Prophetic dreams sometimes feed us information that
is as seemingly incidental and trivial as the dream that
Priestley had of his uncle. But there are just as many
dreams that, when interpreted correctly, can have major
influences on not only this life but the succeeding ones
as well.

I have not had too many dreams that proved prophetic, perhaps because psychic ability lies in other directions. But I would like to relate two dreams of a recurring prophetic nature that I did have.

The first dream is one that I cannot ever remember
not having. It repeated itself throughout my childhood
and into adulthood. In this dream I would find myself
walking through some sort of forest at night. I come
upon a bridge which is curved, arched, and very long.

It seems to have a life of its own, changing shapes and undulating as I begin my journey across it. At times the bridge seems very wide and then it abruptly narrows to a few feet in width. This restricting always unsettles me. The bridge sometimes takes on the exact likeness of the Bronx—Whitestone Bridge, which is a very real struc ture connecting my birthplace (Whitestone, Long Is- land) with the Bronx, the neighboring borough across the East River.

For what seems to be an eternity, I cannot cross over the bridge. There are many side experiences that I have while on this bridge, some of which relate to daily activi- ties, certain fears, and strong desires. Sudden storms arise and I find myself fighting and struggling with high winds, huge waves, and darkened skies. The bridge con- stantly sways during these storms, as if made of rubber. It is a most disorienting feeling. My childhood fear of heights is brought to play here as I am tossed against the railing of the bridge, and when I look down, the water below seems to be miles away.

After what seems like forever, I finally come to the end of the bridge. The road branches off in two directions, and I am confused as to which one I should take. In appearance, they both are the same: black pavement, gutters, and sidewalks lined with trees.

I decide to take the road that bears to the right because I can hear the general sounds of people coming from that direction. The other road is quiet. After walking down the road a way, I come to an area on which there is a very large stage; I walk up the three or four steps that lead onto it. Crossing to the center of the stage, I turn and look out to an audience seated in front of me. There are thousands of people sitting, standing, or crouching. Many balconies are directly behind the audi- ence and these, too, are filled. I begin to do some sort of performing, usually a dramatic song or a very elabo- rate dance.

The audience likes what it sees and hears. They begin to applaud, to yell for more, and to rush toward the stage. Some of them throw flowers and I can see individual faces, all smiling and happy. There is a feeling of complete ecstasy in this dream that I have never experienced when awake. This joyous feeling is almost overpowering.

The crowd wants more; I perform more. This too seems endless. After a time I feel exhausted, drained, trapped. They never let me stop. Ultimately I turn away from them and retreat to the fork in the road, where I sit for awhile on a big rock. The commotion of the audience is ringing in my ears. I look down the second road and discover strange, mist-like lights emanating in the distance. Every now and then I hear a gonglike sound, very low in pitch and vibrating for quite some time. It seems to beckon me toward the beginning of the second road.

I begin to walk down this second road. I keep telling myself that I am only curious about what is at the end of it, that I can always turn around if I don't like what's there, as I did on the first road. After a time I come once again to a stage. This stage is much smaller than the first one. Climbing up the few steps and crossing to its center, I discover that only a handful of people are sitting in front of me. They are on the ground in a semicircle, and I cannot see their faces. I start speaking, but I have never been able to recall what I am saying. I sense that these people are somehow moved by what I am telling them. There is no applause, no sound, but I can feel that they are deeply gratified by whatever it is I am telling them. I somehow perceive from them a completeness and a love that is not physically expressed in any way.

From the distance, I hear the applause and shouting of that first audience in the huge theater. I know that they are beckoning for me to come back. I am suddenly uneasy in front of this overly quiet, nonresponsive few and I rush off the stage, heading back to the first road. The people in the big theater are indeed waiting for me. They go wild with enthusiasm and beg me to sing, to dance, to perform. I please them by doing so. The excitement generated between me and those people is akin to a very deeply experienced sexual gratification.

As I am performing, I begin to think of the few people who made up the second, smaller audience. Something from within me knows that without sound, they are calling me back. I leave the stage with the throngs of people heaping admiration on me as I go. As I get back to the fork in the road I decide to sit. There is the realization that a decision must be made. But, it is torture! Should I go to the audience that has shown such material love? Or, should I take the path that lends to the overly quiet, self-contained few people who sit in the semicircle? I can never make the decision.

I can recall having this dream as far back as age six or seven. It repeated itself in almost the exact same way until well after my thirtieth birthday. It confused me over those years, since I never could decipher its complete meaning. As time progressed, I had bits of understanding afforded me, but only in the last few years have I been able to completely understand its prophetic meaning.

When I was about ten years old, I was taken to the massive Radio City Music Hall in New York City. Instantly, I recognized both the theater and stage as the larger one in my dream. The seating arrangement, with several receding balconies, was exactly the same. This early precognitive experience was unsettling and led me to have an almost supernatural, mystical attraction to the theater. In fact, when I was a teenager, I took a job there just to be close to this place that had so often been a part of my dream experience.

When I first begun having this dream, I had no interest in the theater. But as childhood progressed, I was taken to the movies often by a mother who escaped her own humdrum life in the flickering images. At the age of eleven or twelve I became hooked on the idea of performing. On the surface, I was able to relate to the child performers of the time. In truth, I was searching for a way to get out of a rather lonely, very drab, mostly insecure childhood.

In my late teens I decided that I would be an actor in films or on the stage. Performing in school plays and then in summer stock afforded me moments when I experienced almost the same gratification as I had in my dream. I was fairly successful in a performing capacity, but never completely happy.

It was in my mid-twenties that I turned my interest inward and developed an interest in the supernatural. Latent psychic abilities were brought to the fore, and my career as a professional psychic was begun. Counseling individuals, holding small psychic development classes, lecturing to small groups became a way of life. The second part of my prophetic dream became a reality.

But my need to perform, to make people love me through my entertaining them, was not an easy one to throw off. I was truly torn between my life as a psychic as opposed to one I might have as an entertainer. The interpretation of the dream was complete, and the frustration of never being able to make a decision in the dream was an overpowering truth. Nervous disorders and emotional stress were the outcome. The choice I finally made was to be a psychic, and ironically, through my TV appearances, interviews, and lectures, I have been able to appear on *both* those stages that appear in my dream.

The second dream of a recurring prophetic nature that I have had was one I quickly mentioned in my book *Your Eastern Star*. Although it deals for the most part with the past—a previous life, in fact—there are aspects of prophecy in it.

In this dream I find myself dressed in long, white robes

tied in the middle by a silklike rope. At the beginning of this dream, I am always sitting in the lotus position. Arising, I am aware of walls that seem to be open to the outside. In the distance there is a lovely garden which surrounds a small body of water, possibly a pond.

The plaintive sound of a gong is heard, and I leave the building I am in and set off through a thicket which is made up of unfamiliar vegetation. I move uphill, over an unpaved road or wide path. The land once again becomes flat. A strange building looms up in front of me, painted a very bright orange. As a child I remember referring to it as "the orange Christmas tree house"; its many levels jut out as a pine tree does, one beneath the other, coming to a point at the top.

In the dream I begin walking around the odd house. I can actually smell things in this dream. There is a sense of dampness in the air. The ground is covered with a soft, velvetlike, brilliant green growth. There are several stones of various sizes placed on the green. I choose one and sit on it, putting my hands up to my face. There is a feeling of quiet, of peace. Nothing else ever happens in this repeated dream, other than my sitting with my hands over my face for various periods of time.

I have had this dream over the years and never had the slightest inkling as to its meaning. It was always so pleasant that I made myself have the dream whenever I was depressed or when something negative would occur in my life. The day following this dream always seemed most uplifting—the peaceful, almost joyful mood of the dream would carry over into my waking state for at least twenty-four hours.

It was not until 1970, when I first had the opportunity to visit Japan, and went to the remote island of Miyajima, that my dream came to complete realization.

Everything in the dream was on the island of Miyajima. I had a six-hour *déjà-vu* experience. I discovered the bright orange building—a five-leveled pagoda. There was a path that led uphill from several houses with thatched roofs, one of which I recall as being the house I leave at the start of the dream. The deep green growth I recall in the dream was a brightly colored and heavily textured moss. White stones jutted out of this moss. I did sit for at least an hour on one of those stones and meditated with my hands up to my face.

I realized that I had been living on the island of Miyajima in another life and that my dream gave me awareness to this past life. I knew and recognized everything about the mountainous, relatively unchartered island before I arrived there. I had total recall of being a white-robed Buddhist monk and of going from my home in the temple to the orange pagoda to meditate and pray.

The dream was prophetic in that it wasn't until I was there in *this* life and recognized all that I had seen in my dream that I came to realize the truth of the experience. Had I not had the dream before I got to Miyajima, I doubt whether I would have recognized the place from a past experience. It was as though past, present, and future became one. I fully realized that there is no such thing as time; a most exhilarating, albeit frightening experience.

Dreams can give us insight to past life experiences as well as future. Sometimes elements of past and future are blended together in dreams and reveal more about ourselves than we dare to perceive in a waking state of consciousness.

I have often been able to relate to past life experiences while giving consultations. I recall one particular psychic reading I recently gave. A young woman from New York City came to me quite troubled and concerned about her state of mind.

"I have always felt that I was going to die when I was thirty," she told me. "Since I have been very psychic in many situations regarding myself and my family, this has made me most upset. If that's the case, I only have a few more years . . . and I feel that I will die quite violently."

"Why violently?" I asked.

"I just know it."

"Did you ever stop to think that what you are picking up is from a past life experience?" I inquired of her. "I am sensing that in the life before this one, you were an American Indian. You were pursued by a group of white men who finally caught up with you and shot you in the back, more than once."

The woman shuddered. She stood up and turned, lifting her blouse. On her back were three strange, purple-colored indentations.

"I've always loved anything relating to the American Indians, although I haven't even seen one. And I've had these marks on my back since I was born, although there was no physical reason for them being there. I do have dreams where I am being chased, it seems as though on horseback, but the emotion is so strong that I don't ever see the horse. I do hear gunshots in my dream. For some reason, I have always felt it was a dream relating to the future."

We continued the reading, and I could see that a terrific load had been taken from her. The only thing that still bothered her was that at the conclusion of her dream she had always seen a particular face looking down at her body. The identity of this face was so clear—dark brown hair, a moustache, chiseled features, black eyes, high cheekbones. "I've always felt that this man was going to appear in the future and do me in," she exclaimed. But I got nothing more on it.

About a year later I received a phone call from this young woman. "Mr. Logan, you won't believe what has happened. About three months ago I met a man who was the exact one I have seen in my dream, the man who stands over me. We had this instant feeling of recognition. Had I seen him before I had the reading with you,

I'd have fled in terror. But my interpretation of it was
that he had been one of those that pursued me, for one
reason or another, and killed me. I don't think that he
had the same face then, but I do believe my dream had
some element of prophecy in it. The entire dream was
from the past, except that I saw the man as he would look
today, in *this* life. It is the same face. I would have been
able to recognize it anywhere. He, too, realizes that we
have some karmic tie and we have become real close."

This incident, and many more like it, proves to me how
the subconscious can afford us glimpses of both past and
future events. That is why it is so important for dreams
to be recorded and carefully studied by the individual
who has them. Dreams can offer much more of a reality
than the experiences of our waking state of awareness.

> *For in that sleep of death what dreams may come*
> *When we have shuffled off this mortal coil,*
> *Must give us pause.*

> —*Hamlet,* ACT. III, SCENE I

FIVE

The Good Doctor

Dr. Stanley Padulsky, a chemist and pharmacist by profession, was born in Poland during the latter part of the nineteenth century. The people of the small German city in which he lived and practiced deeply respected the work of this man who had emigrated to their country. Dr. Padulsky was Jewish, so in the 1940's, at the height of the insanity perpetrated on the world by Adolph Hitler, Dr. Padulsky was taken away from his home and placed in a concentration camp. When he refused to do chemical experiments on fellow Jews, he was put to death.

I did not know Dr. Padulsky while he lived. He was brought to my awareness by Deon Frey, a most successful trance medium from Chicago. It was in 1964 that the presence of this entity from another level of existence was made known to me.

I had gone to Deon Frey as a client, seeking her

psychic advice, for my life at that time was filled with confusion and I was in much need of direction. A roommate suggested that I contact Deon after we both had attended a lecture she gave at the New York City's Parapsychology Forum. Subsequent meetings with Deon are detailed in my autobiography; however, this is the first time that I am disclosing the contents of two private trance sessions that I had with her.

I did not mention Dr. Stanley Padulsky in my previous writings for two reasons. First, I wanted to protect him from the kind of negative put-downs I had observed in regard to Fletcher, the spirit "entity" that was said to have worked through medium Arthur Ford. Also, in the 1960's the prevailing attitude toward the realms of the psychic was not yet a positive one by any means. Merely stating that I was a psychic opened up avenues of criticism, skepticism, and ridicule. Times have now changed to the point where I feel that the work I did with Dr. Stanley Padulsky will be taken more seriously than if I had acknowledged him before.

Although I had been introduced to the world of spiritualism as far back as 1958, I had not believed completely in the existence of entities who can contact persons from another level of consciousness. I was neither a skeptic nor an enthusiast, rather choosing to acquire as much evidence as possible before making a decision about the phenomenon which often appears to manifest itself through entities and those they might be able to contact on earth.

It was a very warm day in the early autumn of 1964 that I hurried to keep my first appointment with Deon Frey, who was staying at the apartment of the gifted painter, Wayne Terry, on 57th Street in Manhattan. Deon greeted me at the door and bade me enter the apartment. Her long, red hair and sharply chisled features seemed even more pronounced and startling than when I had seen her on the platform during her lecture.

Deon led me quickly into a room that had been half-darkened. She lit a candle and stretched out on a sofa-bed. She asked me to sing something, as this would "build up the vibrations" in the room. Having become somewhat self-conscious at that point, I could think of only one song, and nervously I sang "Jingle Bells."

After a brief period of silence, I noticed that Deon was drifting into a trancelike state of consciousness. Her body became very rigid and then appeared to become much larger. Deon's hands seemed to double in size.

A voice began to speak to me. It emanated from Deon's mouth, but was decidedly masculine. Her face also took on a kind of masculinity. At first, I attributed this to the glow of the flickering candle, but as time passed, I was convinced that Deon's body, face, mannerisms, and personality had indeed been transformed.

The voice that came from Deon's vocal chords addressed itself in a most friendly manner. It was calm, almost detached, and quite soothing—a complete contrast to the hyper, almost uncontrollable and high-pitched tonal quality of Deon's real voice.

Having had a background in spiritualism, I asked the entity to identify itself. I wanted to make sure that this was a positive energy.

The reply was that Deon's body had been taken over by her spirit guide. The voice told me that he was a man who had lived in the previous century and who had died while in his forties. He also gave me his name, but since I have lost contact with Deon, I do not know whether or not she would wish me to divulge this information.

Deon's entity passed on many prophetic details which over the years have come to pass. This includes my success in the theater, leaving a theatrical career, becoming a renowned psychic, and being the author of various books on the subject of psychic phenomena. At that time, I would have taken bets against any of these things having even a slight chance of happening. Yet not only did they occur, but in the order that Deon's spirit guide told me they would.

After that initial trance session with Deon, I had more than enough to ponder over when I returned home. I had at first been told about spirits and guides back in the late 1950's by Mae Aitken, a very dear lady I had met in Hartford, Connecticut, who was responsible for my interest in psychic phenomena.

Mae Aitken was a spiritualist, and many a night we sat in her living room discussing the spirit world in which she believed so completely. On several occasions I heard strange sounds and rappings coming from different parts of her apartment. At that time, I didn't know whether the lady was somewhat off-balance, a good magician, a true spiritualist, or what. No matter, for it was all quite new and exciting to me, and there was very little else to do in Hartford in those days.

Miss Aitken took me to a local spiritualist church and I had my introduction to the seriousness of dealing with entities from a supposed supernatural world. I was told from spiritualist mediums in that church and others I was to later attend that I had several spirits around me, and a few guides. One of these entities was described by several different mediums. They would tell me that he was always close to me and describe him—fair complexion, short in stature, rather thin and somewhat hunched over, and with a pronounced foreign accent. At that time I felt that, if anyone, this entity must be my mother's father. Later, hearing descriptions of Dr. Stanley, I was to realize that these mediums had accurately sensed the presence of the Polish chemist.

It wasn't until many years after that initial trance session with Deon Frey that I began to investigate the possible existence of spirit guides. While doing research, I discovered that throughout history man has believed in spirits which can come back to guide those on earth. The Egyptians had a history of belief in spirit guides. In fact, from very ancient times, almost all religions have in some way related to entities that hover over and assist those in need. American Indian lore is replete with stories of spirit guides that attach themselves to their earth counterparts during many of their secret, mystical rituals. The Chinese and Japanese cultures are steeped in beliefs of spirit entities that protect and guide the living.

Ghosts, entities, spirits, and all manner of beings from other levels of existence have always made up a major part of the world of literature. What would *Hamlet* be without the prodding, violent, vengeful spirit of Hamlet's father? As we have seen, Shakespeare utilized spirits and their doings in many of his plays, both the comedies and tragedies. Without spirit contact, plays such as *Hamlet, The Tempest, A Midsummer Night's Dream,* Part I *Henry IV, Henry V,* and *Macbeth* all would have little meaning and less motivation.

Having been born a Catholic, I recall that my religious teachings as a child included belief in guardian angels, which were spirits, of course. The Bible has countless allusions to spirits and their works. The Book of Daniel mentions that there are angels and spirits who watch over kingdoms and peoples (Chapters 10 and 12). In Genesis (3:24) it is said that the Garden of Eden was guarded by winged creatures descended from Mesopotamian spirits believed to intercede for men with God. Jesus made many references to spirit guides. The outstanding one is from Matthew (18:10), when he advised his disciples not to despise children. Jesus said, "For I tell you that in heaven their angels [spirit guides] always behold the face of my Father."

Deon Frey's spirit guide was the first experience I had confronting an entity from another level of consciousness. I decided to go back to Deon for a second trance session. This time my questions were in regard to my spiritual progress.

"I would like to know whether or not I have a spirit

guide," I asked. "If I do, can you tell me this spirit's name?"

"Yes," the masculine voice that emanated from Deon emphasized. "You do have a spirit guide and his name is Dr. Stanley Padulsky, but you are to refer to him as Dr. Stanley."

Deon's guide gave me the information concerning Dr. Stanley and then requested that I prepare for trance work myself, "as this will be your spiritual development in the near future. . . . Dr. Stanley will work through you," Deon's spirit guide told me. "He will utilize your body and vocal apparatus to accomplish this. There will be many souls that will be guided by Dr. Stanley. You will learn much from your association with him yourself. You are to be the channel through which Dr. Stanley will work, a vessel for his being."

I didn't respond. I wasn't too thrilled at what I thought might be the possession of my being by an entity from another level of experience. Being a trance medium was the farthest thought from my mind. And, I had attempted a trance once or twice by myself with disastrous results. Not knowing anything about trances, I almost died; friends of mine put me in a cold shower after they could not bring me back from a trance I had put myself into.

"You might now object to this path that you are being placed on," the spirit added, doing some mind reading. "But you will turn to this phase of your experience. It is karmic in nature, this ability to go into trance and allow other forces to enter and assist your fellow man. It is important that you accomplish positive things with your psychic ability in this life."

"Did I misuse my psychic powers in another life?" I asked. It had often been brought to my attention by mediums that I had in some way not utilized my abilities correctly in past lives.

"Let us just say that you allowed yourself to be misguided in past lives, and that this ability you have carried over from other lives is being given another opportunity to emerge. What you do with this ability is of course up to you. We can only make you aware of why you have it and what it is."

It seems I have no choice, I thought.

"Ahh, but you do have a choice." The entity was mind reading again. "You will be rewarded for utilizing your psychic ability in spiritual as well as material ways."

I began to think that Deon's spirit guide was sounding a bit self-righteous and preachy. But I immediately threw that thought out, not wanting him—or Deon's subconscious, if that be the case—to pick up on this impression as well.

This second trance session with Deon came to an end and I departed, somewhat confused by the information afforded me in regard to this new aspect of psychic development. Although I was aware of psychic abilities that were within me since childhood, I had no desire whatsoever to utilize them in a "professional capacity." At that time I still wanted to be an actor.

Deon Frey was to return to New York City several times that year and hold psychic development classes which I attended. One day, while the class was meditating and attempting psychometry, I drifted into a trance and was taken over by an entity. This spirit later turned out to be the mother of Deon's boyfriend, who was earthbound. The group that had gathered for this class gave the spirit enlightenment and, after a subsequent trance, her spirit was released from the bondage it had held itself in by remaining earthbound. I was intrigued by the idea that I had gone into a trance almost against my conscious effort to avoid it. I did not feel anything negative about the experience; in fact, the idea of having assisted a soul that was in desperate need was most positive.

With small groups of friends, I experimented with

trance work and discovered that whoever came to the trance sessions was influenced in some way, and often helped, by what transpired. Assistance was given to everyone who spoke with Dr. Stanley, whether it be spiritual or material. From the beginning, Dr. Stanley has been the entity that first identifies himself at the beginning of every one of these sessions.

Dr. Stanley explained the reason for my introduction to trance mediumship in the manner in which it occurred: "We allowed you to have that initial experience with the earthbound spirit, as we realized that you needed to have an experience that would prove to you our good intent and that what you can experience in trance is not possession. We would not have allowed the entity to work through you as a control if we did not feel that both the spirit and those at the trance session would be equally elevated to more awareness in some way."

The technique for my going into trance seems rather a simple one. Deon Frey was the teacher in trance guidance, and the method I choose to work with is similar to the one she utilizes. There is always meditation before a trance, lifting the vibrations to a higher level by the means of purifying the atmosphere. My trances are done lying prone on a bed or sofa. After a few moments in this position, I begin to have the sensation of my body functions slowing down. My heartbeat is below normal, and my breathing comes in long, drawn-out breaths. Multicolored lights seem to swirl in front of my closed eyes. Then a very soothing sensation occurs of blood rushing to the cheek area of my face. Immediately after this I am out—or more to the point, Dr. Stanley is in.

Often, I do not recall where I am after having been in trance. It is like a deep, comfortable sleep. A few times I have traveled astrally during a trance. Once I was up along the ceiling looking down at the trance session in progress (this had also happened when Deon's boyfriend's mother had been able to utilize my body—I recalled the entire proceedings of that trance, as my conscious mind was hovering above my body taking in everything as an observer).

On yet another occasion, I went into trance and traveled astrally to a place that was quite different from any place I have ever been, consciously or unconsciously. The background of this place was a bright crystal-clear blue. There were three steps leading to a raised area. There were several white-robed men sitting facing me on this dais type of platform. One man in the center was quite prominent and brought to mind a Roman or Greek emperor. He spoke to me about my having patience and doing the right thing in regard to some problems I was going through in reality. It sounded like a sermon and I attempted to object (a habit I have in daily experience). The man in the center would lift his hand up high over his head every time I objected. He would then make a throwing motion and I would see this dazzling, golden ball hurtle through the air. It would hit me in the mouth, and as it did, the ball would become a word. The word was *obedience*. I can remember getting angry and trying to protest this "lesson." This reaction was met with but another ball of gold hitting me in the mouth.

It all seems rather like some melodramatic science fiction story now, but it wasn't very funny when I came out of that trance and the two friends I was with, Lisa Gladstone and Bill McCarthy, discovered that my mouth was swollen and bleeding! I don't know if having one's lessons hurtled through the air and striking one directly in the mouth is a good way of learning, but I do know that I was a bit more careful in listening and not objecting to anything or anyone for quite some time.

Usually I awaken from a trance in a kind of daze, akin to a hangover from alcohol or drugs. There is a strange combination of both exhaustion and euphoria. According to the status of my physical health at the time of the trance, I am either replenished with more energy after

a trance or completely drained. The better my health,
the better the trance. If I am not well when I go into
trance, I usually feel much worse afterwards. I try to
build up my physical as well as psychic energies before
I go into trance.

Many of my first group trance sessions were held at
the home of Grace Gearhart, a psychic who lives in
Brooklyn, New York. These sessions were quite elevated
in their spiritual nature and content, probably because
most of the group that attended them were very progressed in matters of awareness. Listening to the tapes
I kept of the Brooklyn trances and those that were held
later in my office and at the home of Miss Clara Hoover
in New York City, I can see that Dr. Stanley was not
interested in the run-of-the-mill kind of seance, with ec-
toplasm and trumpets appearing and disappearing. Dr.
Stanley's purpose was to offer guidance to the individual
and the group as a whole.

Dr. Stanley foretold the 1974 energy crisis seven years
before it happened. He kept warning persons who attended the trance sessions to make sure that "you have
enough dry goods and candles in your homes over the
next ten years as there will be many blackouts of elec-
tricity, some that will last for long periods of time." No
one who attended the group sessions was much surprised when the first big power failure took place in
November 1965. They were looking for it to happen.
There was no precedent for such an occurrence, nothing
material to base this prophecy on, although brownouts
and blackouts have since become a way of life for most
of us who live on the East Coast of the United States.
I can recall those in the group wondering *how* the blackouts would happen; whether or not beings from out of
space would create the problems.

Until recently I have had little concern for politics,
science, or the world of economics. In the early days of
my career as a trance medium, I held no regard for any

of these subjects. That they existed was about the level of my caring to understand anything about them. Dr. Stanley, on the other hand, showed a keen interest in these subjects and constantly made prophecies about them while I was in trance.

Upon playing the tapes back and in going over much of the material in my autobiography* that I culled from them, I discover a degree of accuracy in Dr. Stanley's prophecies concerning world events that is quite staggering.

In a trance session dated 1966, Dr. Stanley said: "The years ahead for the United States are not pleasant ones to look forward to. The war in Vietnam will continue for at least several years, well into the 1970's, and it will grow in intensity. Although it may be brought to a temporary halt for political reasons just before the 1968 elections, the war will break out again shortly after that, if not in Vietnam itself, then in another section of Southeast Asia."

As we all too well know, that infamous war did extend into the 1970's, and it did grow in intensity. Dr. Stanley's prophetic awareness that President Johnson would bring the war to a "temporary halt" (cease fire) just before the 1968 elections is so accurate as to be startling. And the war did break out again and involved other Southeast Asian countries, such as Cambodia.

Dr. Stanley made me completely aware of politics and it was through the trance sessions that I geared myself toward a more liberal attitude, after having been somewhat to the Right for most of my youth. (I recall having youthful, misguided pride in Senator Joseph McCarthy's Communist witch-hunting.)

Another of Dr. Stanley's statements regarding the war was taken from a succeeding tape: "The war in Vietnam could have been brought to a conclusion long before it

* The Reluctant Prophet (Doubleday, 1968)

will be. Those involved prolong the war for their own political or financial gain. It will continue into the 1970's."

I would use the information given to the class by Dr. Stanley at my public lectures, stating that the war was indeed wrong and that if not stopped, it could ruin the country. Many spiritual and parapsychological organizations banned me from their platforms during the period from 1966 to 1967. One lady in charge of a well-known Forum in New York City said: "I will not have you using my spiritual Forum for politics. Tonight was the last lecture you can give here. We must stand behind the government. I don't know where you get your information from, but you've lost a large number of potential customers [for psychic consultations] because of your misinformed political leanings. The war in Vietnam should not be brought up at spiritual meetings. God is good, and this country is good. We are doing the right thing!"

My life was threatened several times by persons accusing me of being un-American for my statements against the war, given to me by Dr. Stanley while I was in trance. These incidents made me do a lot of thinking about the true spirituality of many such philosophical and spiritually oriented groups.

Dr. Stanley told the classes about the breakdown in the country long before it began to occur. He warned those who attended the trances: "The Nixon regime will not be a positive one. Great unrest will hit the country on every level. There will be many upheavals; much violence will erupt; this man and those under him are not to be trusted."

Dr. Stanley did not think that the Kennedy dynasty were the saviors of the country either. Although he did feel that John F. Kennedy was an honest man who tried to do his best, he had little if no positive feelings about Robert Kennedy. As for Ted Kennedy, Dr. Stanley said that "right now [1968] all I can do is snicker at the thought of Ted Kennedy in charge of your country. But, given time and his choices, I will reserve my complete feelings until at least five to ten years' time."

In a trance session in fall of 1965, several statements made by Dr. Stanley shock me now in retrospect because his awareness of what would take place in the country was so on target: "Inflation faces your country by 1968. In the early 1970's there will be a depression in which many small businesses will fail. From 1968 on, strikes, rises in prices, and a shortage of employment will prevail in the United States."

Dr. Stanley's deadly accuracy in regard to world situations, made years before any unrest was even evident, still amazes me. I would never have dared to utter these prophetic statements, had they not been received while I was in trance. Frankly, at the time I heard them on the tapes, I did not have much confidence that the events would happen. (Unfortunately for the country, they have.) Many of the prophecies Dr. Stanley gave while I was in trance actually went against my own beliefs, impressions, and feelings about certain matters. I recall coming out of several trances and raising objections to prophecies made by Dr. Stanley. "He didn't *really* say that?" I would remark.

But I did have faith in Dr. Stanley. I was aware that this entity knew more about everything than I did, and although several of his prophecies seemed outrageously farfetched, my complete trust in him gave me the confidence to utilize the predictions in my lecturing and during appearances on the various media.

One of the prophecies that Dr. Stanley made in regard to medicine (October 24, 1966) raised much controversy when it was included in my autobiography: "If I were to tell you that there already exists a cure for certain cancers, would you believe it? There is such a cure, but it has been suppressed by persons in both your government and medical associations for the sake of money that is being received by doctors and hospitals that treat cancer victims."

This statement came after a previous trance in which Dr. Stanley said: "In the years before the twenty-first century, cures for major illnesses will be discovered. Many forms of cancer will be found to be preventable or curable. The causes of some cancers will be found to be a virus."

As happy as I was to learn of the prophecy that a breakthrough in cancer research would be forthcoming in my own lifetime, I was dismayed when Dr. Stanley broke the news that certain factions in both medical and governmental organizations were in some way withholding the cancer preventions or cures.

The media also seemed dismayed about this prophecy, and many criticisms were launched against my autobiography for having included it therein:

"How could you make such a statement?"

"Don't you have any sense of responsibility? Think of all those who are suffering with cancer, and their families. What will they feel when they read this prediction?"

"Do you really expect us to believe that government or medical associations would be so cruel as to join in some kind of a pact to hold back a breakthrough in this field for monetary gain?"

These questions and others like them were flung at me from the press, TV and radio hosts, and magazine writers. It was the one prediction that I almost regretted having made. No matter how kindly disposed a critic might be toward me and my work, this one prophecy alienated him against the book and myself.

But my trust in Dr. Stanley is 100 percent, and I wasn't going to pick and choose prophecies that seemed "safe" and those that didn't upset the general atmosphere of known factors. I did not exactly know how to answer my critics back then. I just knew that it must be so if it came from Dr. Stanley. Today I could very easily answer these critics in light of the scandals that have rocked not only our government but the medical field as well.

Dr. Stanley warned the class members of the stock market situation and the country's general financial outlook (which at the time seemed most secure). "The value of all monies shall decrease. This will happen first in England. Be careful in your investments, for during the years from 1968 on, the stock market will have ups and downs, but mostly downs, and many an investor will fail. The 1970's will be most negative in regard to your country's financial situation."

In October 1965, Dr. Stanley answered a question put to him by a class member about the continuing drought which was gripping the northeastern area of the United States. He said that the devastating drought would shortly end and that "from the early part of 1967 through the fall of that year, there will be unusually heavy snowfalls, violent storms, and torrential rainfalls. Floods, rather than drought, will then become the problem."

The fantastic amount of precipitation that began in 1967 did indeed end the drought, and in succeeding trances, Dr. Stanley's continuous references about changes in weather have also seen fruition. "There will be less and less difference in the changes of seasons. Spring and fall will almost not exist in coming years. You will go from extremely cold weather into unbearably hot, humid weather conditions. Spring and fall clothing will be a thing of the past. Electrical power failures will make the situation even worse than it is."

The weather conditions have changed over the past few years exactly as Dr. Stanley prophesied. Weatherwise, we go from one extreme to the other.

June 11, 1965: "It is confusing to us on the other side

as to the tremendous interest in the moon that your scientists have. It does appear that far too much time, money, and effort are being utilized in the 'space race.' Your country will be the first to walk on the moon, to analyze its composition, and to return to its surface more than once. But, far better to place some of that energy into the investigation of healing factors regarding disease and well-being.

"As I have repeated before, disease—all disease—is first accepted in the mind before it can be generated in the physical body. The control of this aspect of the mind should be the next area of scientific investigation. As it is, not until near the twenty-first century will your scientists seriously take up methods of psychic healing, acupuncture, yoga, and other natural healing methods. They will be too busy with the moon and the oceans of the earth to realize that much of their efforts are misplaced energy."

January, 1966: "Natural catastrophes, in the United States as well as other parts of the world, will be much in evidence. The climatic changes now occurring in the world will become more noticeable. The climate of the earth will be one of extremes of heat and cold. The reason for this is that the earth has been moved almost imperceptibly off its previous axis by the detonation of atomic weapons, and those which have been exploded under the surface of the earth are those that have done the most damage. If explosions of this nature continue, the earth will be shifted from its axis more each time it is done."

Dr. Stanley was to tell members of the classes that there would be race riots on the West Coast in 1967, that Russia and the United States not only would become friendly disposed toward each other but would be closely allied, and mentioned many other events that have since become reality. Although many of these prophecies seem negative, I do believe that Dr. Stanley was attempting to give warning to those of us who would listen to his words. It was in the realms of dealing with the individuals who made up the classes that Dr. Stanley offered upliftment and courage and expressed a prophetic ability that was uncanny.

SIX

Guidance and Enlightenment

Dr. Stanley was to offer demonstrations of his interest in medicine and chemistry in the most unusual way. During one session he asked that "each person attending the meeting place a glass of water under or near his seat prior to the trance." When asked why, Dr. Stanley simply stated that it was important to do so and that the reason would be made evident at the meeting.

When the group met the following week, everyone got a glass of water and placed it on the floor next to his chair. I had no idea what Dr. Stanley was up to, and I must admit to being somewhat concerned, knowing that with such a large group—fourteen—there was bound to be at least one spilled glass of water on my Oriental rug.

During the trance Dr. Stanley explained: "Each of you has a different chemical makeup in your body. Some of you lack certain substances in the body which would help to bring about more harmonious conditions regarding health. While you have been here, I have added the missing chemicals, substances, or combinations thereof, which will assist your body to commence functioning properly. You will notice changes in color and taste in the individual glasses of water. Do not drink another person's water, as this will tend to throw off you body's health even more, creating further problems with the imbalances of poor and bad foods that all of you seem to eat continually."

After this trance, when I was slowly brought to consciousness—a transition that takes from about five to fifteen minutes, according to how deep I have gone—everyone was excited about their water. Each glass did appear different in color, ranging from a milky gray to a greenish yellow. Some of the liquids in the glasses had thickened. But all the water had been drawn from the same tap, by the class members themselves, just before the class began.

Some of the group did not want to drink their "prescribed liquid." I remember Karen Dent saying, "It looks so very strange, I don't know if I can put my lips to it."

"Ughhh!" cried Karen's mother, Eileen. "This stuff tastes almost vile. What the hell does my body lack that I have to have *this?*"

"Mine smells and tastes like sulfa or slightly turned hard-boiled eggs," Noel Whitman exclaimed.

Eleanor Titian said that hers was overly sweet, and Mildred Sullivan felt that there had been little if any change from the tap water she usually drinks. Some of the group felt that their water had a lemon flavor. One actually could not drink it at all, stating that it tasted as though dead fish had been it it. Ronnie Saladino said that his was delicious and tasted like a health food drink.

I must state here that I am not a particular advocate of "psychic manifestations" or materializations which set out to prove that the world of the spirit does exist. These phenomena have been faked so often, and indeed they are not necessary—either one believes or one does not. I never could understand why a *physical* materialization was accepted as evidence of a *spiritual* existence.

The changing of the water was a manifestation that was accomplished by an entity to directly help those it had come in contact with, rather than to denote some sensational phenomena. I recall that one or two in the group did not particularly believe that the changing of the water had been done by an outer force, although they knew that there had been no physical way to change fourteen glasses of water into fourteen different liquids by me or anyone else in the group.

In succeeding weeks the water was always changed for those present into different tasting and textured liquids. In my own case, the water that Dr. Stanley prepared for me was almost foul tasting, like a combination of cod liver oil, oranges, and sulfa. The first time I cheated by drinking only half the glass and hoping that nobody would see me. Try as I did, I just couldn't get the stuff down. One of the group had been aware of this, however, and jokingly asked in private, "Can't take some of your own medicine, huh?"

Those persons who have had direct contact with Dr. Stanley are always aware of the utter difference in personality between Dr. Stanley and myself when in a non-trance state of consciousness. The slight accent and very different phrasing of sentences are the physical changes, but it is Dr. Stanley's manner that is so at odds with my own.

Eileen Dent, who had once been my secretary and who was present at many trance sessions, has verbalized it best: "Daniel, I know that it isn't you when you go into trance. Dr. Stanley approaches everything from a completely different angle than you do. His entire viewpoint and character seem really at odds with your own. His patience and understanding are on a level that cannot be compared with yours. Even when you give consultations, your manner and approach are unlike that of Dr. Stanley. I suppose that an entity from another plane of existence would have a different approach and feeling about things than us mortals, but there are times when I am made so aware of his energy, which is entirely different from yours."

Some people are batteries for recharging psychic energy, and Eileen Dent is one for me. I always garner a tremendous shot of both physical and mental energy when she is near. (It was that way with my friend Mae Aitken as well.) I try not to meditate when Eileen is around, for I find myself going off into trance despite my attempts not to.

Eileen and I were at the home of Joan Cloutier in Rochester, getting ready for a lecture, and the three of us were meditating. Suddenly, I went off into trance without any knowledge of having done so. What seemed like a fraction of a second in time, I was told, had been more than twenty minutes. Dr. Stanley took over and gave prophecies to both Eileen and Joan. He also gave a few about me for them to relate upon my coming out of trance.

Dr. Stanley told Joan that she would soon lose her sister and that she must be prepared to do something about her nephew. Her sister did die, and the child was subsequently taken care of.

Eileen and I both work as psychic energizers for Joan Cloutier, since when she is in meditation with us, a strange phenomenon takes her over. She loses control of her hands and they act as separate entities, lifting themselves quite against her will. She has been most embarrassed by this in public meetings, as her arms take on the appearance of being controlled by puppet strings and hover for long periods of time above her head and directly out in front of her. It is a strange manifestation, but it is there. It is my belief that she is meant to do something with her hands—something that will utilize this energy, such as psychic healing.

Jean Dominico, a young lady who attended some of my psychic awareness classes, was assisted by Dr. Stanley in locating the area for and building a home. She was one of the persons who talked with spirits that utilized my speaking apparatus other than Dr. Stanley. (To be sure, it was Dr. Stanley who allowed these other spirits to use me thus.)

"Jean," Dr. Stanley said, "I have a relative here with me from the spirit world. He wishes to talk with you."

Jean accepted this and what transpired was a conversation between herself and an uncle—all in Italian! Now let it be known that my own knowledge of the Italian language is limited to a few pleasantries such as "hello" and "goodbye," and several phrases that couldn't be used in public. The tapes of this communication between Jean and her uncle are very light, easy, and filled with a kind of joy that is apparent in the voices of Italians who have not seen each other in some time.

There was only one occasion when an entity that was indeed negative came into my body. I had been giving some of my classes at the home of Clara Hoover on Park Avenue in New York City. Miss Hoover had utilized my psychic ability on several occasions when persons had been "ripping her off." One instance became a famous scandal in the late 1960's when through trance sessions, Dr. Stanley exposed this lady's lawyer and masseuse as having negotiated to relieve her of some large amount of money.

On this particular evening in Miss Hoover's apartment I had been having some difficulty going into trance. I had been ill during the day and was exhausted. I wanted to cancel the class, but knew that it would entail getting too many people on the phone. It being such short notice, I knew I probably would not be able to contact all of them anyway, so I went under against my better judgment.

From the tapes I have heard of this trance, there was much discomfort expressed by both the class members and myself. Dr. Stanley's voice was distant and quivering. The vessel he was utilizing to get through was not in perfect working order. The time it took for me to get into trance and the long stretches of silence on the tape are indicative of a session that should not have been held. Previous to this trance, Dr. Stanley had told Miss Hoover in private sessions that it was the spirit of the masseuse's husband who indeed had been the culprit. The man had chosen to remain on the earth plane and to use his wife as a direct channel for his misdeeds. He had had an extremely negative vibration while he lived, and the stories that the masseuse told Miss Hoover of his life were indeed those of a most adverse soul.

Listening to the tapes, one can see that a struggle was somehow ensuing between Dr. Stanley and another entity. The class became quite frightened, and when the masseuse's husband identified himself by screaming out his name, they began to pray for his soul. After a few moments, there was silence. Suddenly a sound that pierced the semi-darkened room made the entire group cringe with fear. In some way, the negative entity that had taken over my vocal chords began to rip the back of the couch I was lying on, from one end to the other. It was a most horrifying sound.

"We've got to say some prayers or something," my deeply concerned friend, Bill McCarthy shouted, attempting to gain control of the class members who were anxiously stirring about. "Don't anyone move, please, sit still!"

"Should I switch on the light?" Miss Hoover asked.

"No," Bill exclaimed, "it might be too much of a shock for Daniel."

The sound of the sofa being torn became louder, and the entity began to shout obscenities. From listening to the tapes, I can truthfully state that these sounds were not unlike some of those that emanated from the young girl who was possessed in *The Exorcist*.

Bill felt that the vibrations must be built up immediately, that Dr. Stanley was there in the background but that because of the poor state of physical health I was in, the negative force had been given an opportunity to emerge, take over, and begin its own work.

"Let's sing," Bill shouted above the din. The class quickly chose the hymn "Nearer My God to Thee," the song sung during the sinking of the *Titanic*, meant to build up the vibrations during that strange experience. After several stanzas of this singing, the sound of the couch being ripped became softer and lasted for only short intervals. Ten minutes later, there was silence. Dr. Stanley spoke in a barely audible voice, telling the group to end the session, that, "Daniel will be all right, but should never be allowed to go into trance under these circumstances again. He could be permanently damaged."

I came out of that trance very slowly. I had the most splitting headache. It was difficult to even pick up my head. I finally got up and went directly to the bathroom, where I threw up for quite some time. Oddly enough, I had not eaten very much that day, but I spewed forth enough material matter as though I had eaten several gigantic meals. It was truly horrible.

Never again would I go into a trance without knowing that I was in completely good health—mental as well as physical. In fact, this one experience led me to do less and less deep trance work and express more semi-trance states of consciousness. It was an experience that has haunted me ever since. For years after that I conjured up the image of that trance session immediately prior to going under. If I didn't believe in the protection of Dr. Stanley, I would never have gone into a trance again.

I have come to the conclusion that there are entities that retain certain negative aspects from their most previous incarnation. Dr. Stanley explained to the class that when one dies, he does not automatically become an angel. If there was much negation on the earth plane, it would continue upon the soul's reaching the next plane. Choices could be made by the soul at any level of experience, of course, but it stands to reason that a soul steeped in the negative cannot see the light here or in the hereafter.

According to Dr. Stanley, Adolph Hitler continued to assert the most negative vibrations when he reached the other side. Considering all the adverse choices Hitler made while on earth, I do not think that he would have been able to make immediate positive choices upon his entering the next level of soul experience.

Shakespeare wrote at length of spirits that hover over some of his leading characters and are most destructive to them. I have always thought that Hamlet's father was a negative entity. His goading of Hamlet to commit revengeful acts is but one aspect of this hostile soul. The conversation between Horatio, Bernardo, and Marcellus immediately following the entity's disappearance after its initial manifestation proves Shakespeare's intent to show it as an evil presence:

> MARCELLUS: 'Tis gone!
> We do it wrong, being so majestical,
> To offer it the shew of violence;
> For it is, as the air, invulnerable,
> And our vain blows malicious mockery.
> BERNARDO: It was about to speak when the cock crew.
> HORATIO: And then it started like a guilty thing
> Upon a fearful summons. I have heard,
> The cock, that is the trumpet to the morn,
> Doth with his lofty and shrill-sounding throat
> Awake the god of day; and at his warning,

> Whether in sea or fire, in earth or air,
> The extravagant and erring spirit hies
> To his confine. . . .

MARCELLUS: It faded on the crowing of the cock.
> Some say that ever against that season
> comes
> Wherein our Saviour's birth is celebrated,
> The bird of dawning singeth all night
> long;
> And then, they say, no spirit dare stir
> abroad;
> The nights are wholesome; then no
> planets strike,
> No fairy takes; nor witch hath power
> to charm,
> So hallowed and so gracious is that time.

The military garb it is dressed in, the violent language it uses, and its malicious outburst when it is in the cellarage beneath the stage are evidence that the soul of Hamlet's father is indeed a negative one. Hamlet's father is the cause of not only his son's madness and eventual death, but the deaths of the other characters who expire in the play. It is a revengeful and violent soul, very selfish in bringing about a peace of mind for itself at the expense of his family and former friends.

Shakespeare also shows us that spirits do have the power of choice when it prevents Hamlet from driving Gertrude (the entity's wife) to repentance and urges Hamlet to meditate only upon revenge on Claudius.

Again, there have been those scholars over the past several hundred years who have stated that the ghost of Hamlet's father is merely some stage device, thrown in to make dramatic statements and to lend the stage some sensational effect. This is ridiculous. Shakespeare meant for Hamlet's father to provide the entire motivation for the play. The quite often foolish, selfish, and noncaring Hamlet would never have been moved to do any of the things he does without the awareness brought to him by his father's spirit. It is the spirit's enlightening of situations, past and future, that causes Hamlet to act in the manner he does.

The entities that are conjured up by the three witches in *Macbeth* are also of a negative nature, as they know that Macbeth will wrongly interpret their prophecies, and so be motivated to leave himself open to death by the hand of Malcolm.

The spirit of the husband of the masseuse who had entered my weakened body and mind had been of a like nature. It expressed itself through the wife, who does not completely recall committing the extensive damage she did in regard to Miss Hoover. Miss Hoover and her masseuse had utilized the Ouija Board when the negative force broke through, causing Miss Hoover to separate from her family and give up sums of her money to those on this side who had become aligned with the entity. Miss Hoover was taken in because the negative spirit did indeed give her several prophecies that saw immediate fruition, and so she could not help but believe in the force completely.

The earlier plays of Shakespeare tell of spirits that amuse, play gentle tricks on, or assist those mortals they come in contact with. As Shakespeare grew in understanding of the true nature of the hereafter, he wrote of the negative spirits that also can come back and continue acting in a like manner.

At this point, I would hasten to add that for many years, even after the initial trance sessions with Deon and those I proceeded to do myself, I was not completely convinced that spirits or entities did in fact enter and use my being. I was not at all sure that the condition wasn't a split in my own personality which surfaced during an altered state of consciousness. My acceptance finally came after having listened to tapes I made during trances and after speaking with those who witnessed trance sessions. The communicated material, which I must say is vast, is in most cases not only alien to my own level of awareness, but far superior to my own degree of knowledge in almost any area one may wish to mention.

I was not at all surprised to discover that many mediums of recent times have also questioned whether or not entities did take over their consciousness while they were in the state of trance. Eileen Garrett questioned this point throughout most of her writings, and it wasn't until later in life that she came to completely believe that her control, Uvani, was indeed a personality separate from her own.

In her book, *My Life As a Search for the Meaning of Mediumship,** Mrs. Garrett wrote that Hewat McKenzie was the only leader in the spiritualist movement who directly refused to take any prophecy or pronouncement of a control (spirit) personality as the word of some "higher power." McKenzie explained to Mrs. Garrett that a control personality is merely the interpreter of that which reaches him from other states of consciousness. It was his contention that the entity had to be taught how to make the purest utilization of his powers whatever they be, and to transmit only that which it might receive from the very highest levels of awareness and truth.

I realize now that I have been most fortunate in having Dr. Stanley work through me. I have come across mediums who have permitted the takeover of their consciousness by limited personalities who were themselves in much need of awareness and training. That Dr. Stanley's purpose was to assist not only the individuals who made up the small group classes, but all of mankind as well, is evident in the most recent trances I held. I have herewith transcribed them from the tape, exactly as it was recorded.

* New York: Garrett, 1929.

Date: June 21, 1974
Time: 10:00 A.M.
Place: New York

Good morning, this is Dr. Stanley. It has been a long time, far too long. Yet, I understand why you have not gone into trance of late. But the time is right to start again, Daniel. You have gone through the experiences that were meant for you, and you have grown because of them. This is only the beginning of the battle. Those of you who are meant to guide, instruct, or enlighten in some way—and there are countless many—have gone through the fire and brimstone over the past several years. This is a strengthening effect so that you will not fall when you will be needed by those who will scream with fear and terror in the streets, those who will seek any crumb of awareness. That is why we are making ready so many teachers, guides, healers, and those who will be able to afford some comfort and enlightenment. . . . The time is at hand. . . .
[*Long pause*]

Throughout the earth plane's history, those of you whom we have chosen as a means of communication between ourselves and the souls who are on the earth have been accused of being prophets of doom. . . . [*Slight pause*] You must remember that any of the prophecies we have given you since the existence of the earth plane could have been avoided if the right choices had been made. . . . Nothing except karmic situations are afforded to earth-plane souls, and it is what you choose as a reaction to certain prophetic opportunities which makes the difference. The problem is presented; the solving of that problem is left to the individual soul . . . to any given problem there is a correct answer, an incorrect answer, and several answers that can be either right or wrong under certain circumstances. Only now, of recent time, have your mathematicians come to see the fact that one plus

one does not *always* make two. It is the same with
problems that are presented for soul evolvement
. . . opportunity or prophecy is merely presented.
Unfortunately, many choose to ignore the opportunity itself—run away from it, or in some manner
get rid of it before they have a chance to face
it. . . .

Do you believe that it is a coincidence that you
[*Daniel Logan*] have been brought into the vibration
of Tam Mossman [*The editor of this book*]? It was
through the energy of Seth* and myself that you
were brought together again, having had a most
difficult relationship in a previous incarnation. It
was Tam who pointed you in the direction of this
book, as at the time you first contemplated writing
again, you had completely different ideas on what
the book should be. It was through Tam's guidance, who in turn was guided by those of us on this
level of awareness, that the opportunity of doing
this book was presented to you. Through much difficulty, you grasped the opportunity head on and
have proceeded in the manner that is most correct
for your understanding at this time. Thank you for
accepting us once again. [*About a two-and-a-half-
minute pause*]

Now, you must immediately understand that the
time we have been speaking of over the past few
hundred years is at hand. The spiritualization of the
earth plane is imminent and must be accomplished
within the next ten to twenty years. The time is
now. The catharsis is at hand . . . the millennium
will follow. [*Slight pause*]

Do you believe that the powers of negation that
have infiltrated the most high positions of office on
the earth plane are coincidental? As we prophesied
through you almost ten years ago, the leaders of
your countries will become more materialistic and

---

* Seth is the spirit guide of medium Jane Roberts. Tam Mossman is the
editor of Ms. Roberts' many books, including *The Seth Material* and *Seth
Speaks*, two of the best books on the subject of trance work ever published

self-motivated, more violent and hateful . . . deceit
and mistrust . . . and, remember that they are a direct reflection of the states of mind of the majority
of peoples who place the negative ones in charge
. . . misguided, misdirected energies . . . [*Long
pause*]

We are not as concerned over the black magicians and the devil worshipers as you yourself have
been in recent years, although your previous work
[*America Bewitched*] was indeed important to those
who were not yet aware or initiated in the various
processes of soul evolvement. You, Daniel, have
been upset by the response to that work, as many
misunderstood the point and felt you had immersed
yourself in the very aspects of black magic. You
were guided to do this work, as you know, and the
results of the book being published, plus the other
books and articles by other writers, have been of
value, for it was directly because of these attacks
that several organizations have not only revamped
their ideology, but have openly thrown off the
negative aspects that motivated them. The newspaper articles in the past few weeks should have
brought some feeling of accomplishment to you,
Daniel.*

It is the ill-equipped, ideologically confused
speakers of so-called *wisdom* that we are most concerned with . . . the false prophets . . . the anti-
Christs, which walk the earth plane at this time.

We cannot accept the vibrations that are created
by those who chose to cop out and sit alone on
mountaintops or otherwise shroud themselves in
the seeming protection of a commune. . . . they are
as misguided as those who strive for only material
gain and who are in the very midst of your societies

---

* Dr. Stanley is referring to the recent headlines that The Process Church,
a vast organization which preached that one must know the Devil, Satan, a
negative energy, in order to comprehend God, had thrown out its "high
priest" and denounced its former attachment to the negative energies—Satan, Lucifer, etc.

. . . [*Pause*] Extremes . . . [*Pause*] Extremes bring
about the best possible chance of the negative
prophecies seeing fruition. . . . The acceptance of
negative energies which motivate thousands of
souls is fast taking precedence on the earth plane.
What can we feel of one such as Billy Graham, to
whom we entrusted the ability to become an emis-
sary for the most positive accomplishments, one
who is karmically responsible for the souls of millions, and one who chose the easy way? Why did he
not speak out against the death and destruction
that occurred in Southeast Asia over the past
twenty years? He has indeed turned hundreds of
thousands toward the Light, but does he not see
that so many of these stepped away from the awareness he presented to them when they discovered
him to be immersed in the vibrations of selfish,
negative heads of state? What is to be hoped when
one so evolved chooses not to see? Is it not interesting to you that over the past recent years, Billy
Graham developed a most strange and almost disastrous eye disease, highly reported in your media?
Could this not be a sign of his refusal to see the
truth? Or that he was closing his eyes to certain
situations? We are interested to know what he will
make of new opportunities that are presently being
presented to him. It will be his choice. . . . [*Short
pause*]

There are those who come from the East as well
who profess spiritual qualities, but who in truth are
motivated by material gain . . . which in itself is
not bad or evil—except when it is at the expense of
the progress of any soul in a spiritual, mental, or
physical way.

For hundreds of liftetimes we have prepared the
young one who in this life was born in India. We
groomed him to give of the Light, and in past incarnations he did so. It was in this life that he was
to reach the apex and assist the masses in throwing
off the materialism, the lies of centuries . . . in or-

der that they might better be able to meet the millennium. . . . Even such an advanced soul had the
power of choice, and he chose the material way
. . . an example that has destroyed the faith of
thousands. As they grovel and search out the
crumbs of spiritual and material existence, he rides
not one but many private vehicles, in the air and on
the ground . . . has amassed a fortune in wealth . .
. even this in itself is not negative . . . but his
gross materialism has duly affected his showing of
the Light. . . .

The false prophets are upon you!

And speaking of choice, we are aware of those
who speak for the truth despite the outcome, despite the heartbreak and material loss that will be
theirs.

Example: The soul known as Jane Fonda. This
soul was steeped in materialistic ways for many incarnations. She had the position of power, but
misused it previous to this lifetime. She was placed
in a position in this incarnation that would have
turned many another to the materialistic way. At
the expense of material gain, at the expense of the
hatred of many, at the expense of giving up her
own life, Jane Fonda made choices that were correct, spiritual and, for her, completely true. If she
helped to bring the unspiritual war to a close for
one day, even one hour—helping to save even one
life—then her karma has been paid . . . and she
has paid it many times over. . . .

"Ahhh!" I can hear certain of your readers at this
point . . . *"Stop preaching! Who needs this preaching? It
is the preaching that has turned us off from previous religious cant!"*

If the truth be preaching. . . . but rather look on
it as teaching, direction, and care . . . for above all
else, we *do* care. And of course, there are those who
say, why Daniel Logan? Why has he the ability to
be given this direct communication? If that were

only so, Daniel, you would not be in the constant
turmoil you continually get into. We work through
Daniel Logan *despite* the many vibrations which are
not of a highly elevated caliber. We choose those
who have developed awareness in previous lives.
And Daniel has developed mediumistic abilities in
all his previous lifetimes, although not always in a
positive way. . . . Any of you can communicate with
us directly. You are all mediums if you would but
accept that as fact. But each of you must throw off
the fear, distrust, and misconceptions of past incarnations in order to communicate with us directly.
There will be a time when you will be able to contact us directly in a physical way through inventions
that will break the barriers which separate the
physical earth vibrations from those on our plane of
consciousness. Seth, myself, and others now work
to bring these inventions to the awareness of your
scientists, who now realize that communication is
not only possible but most probably within the next
generation. . . .

But you must first get rid of the vibrations that
have held you in bondage . . . do you not realize
that this is the true reason why the media [*film*] ver-
sions of *The Exorcist* have been so popular, and that
the one other most popular has been *The Godfather?*
The Godfather showed the gross materialization of
the earth plane over the past hundred years . . . in
some way, you have all been a part of the Mafia—
the stealing, the destruction, the hatred and noncaring except for the material exemplified in *The Godfather* was a reflection of not only your own country,
but all the countries of the world—even those in
the East that have had thousands of years of
spiritual progress, such as Japan. *The Exorcist* is in
truth the very exorcism or throwing off of these destructive, material ways. It is not chance that the
young have flocked to see the film. The carnage,
the blood, the obscenities, the disrespect for human

life have become a way of existence with earth-plane experiences. There isn't one aspect of *The Exorcist* that every child on your earth plane has not come into contact with, in one form or another. Subconsciously, the film exorcises these material, ugly manifestations of lives that have chosen the negative path. It is not coincidence that when we worked through the author of this book, we had him choose a young, quite simple and ordinary young girl [*as his central character*]. You are all Regan; you have been "possessed" by the material gain that has confronted you. It is now time to exorcise this aspect of life, throw off the negative, earthbound vibrations. How important to realize that the negative aspects of Christianity are exorcized as well—the guilt of the priest, the bondage that parents hold over the young, the ridiculous aspect of spoken religious cant as opposed to truth, which can never be exorcised. The author, against many of his own wishes, was utilized as a vessel for us to enter into and express our feelings. In turn that is why the reflection in the media of the 1930's and 1940's immediately followed . . . once the devil was exorcized, where does one go? The present is too fraught with the residue of this materialization; the future seems to be an even more difficult time, and so it is in the past that is the only avenue of escape . . . the recent past when things did seem more positive and hopeful, even though materially it was more difficult, what with the poverty and general lack. But the spirit of the Thirties and Forties is what attracts the young to nostalgia.

There is a probable prophecy that another atomic bomb will be dropped again on thousands of persons on the earth plane. Yes, I know that we had earlier predicted that another bomb would *not* be dropped on innocent souls, but again, the choices have been negative . . . for a time it appeared to us that these choices would be positive, even though it would be out of fear and not love that a bomb would not be dropped. But the radical elements, the extremes, are each creating minds that do not care how many are killed, as long as their own selfish and misguided way of thinking is appeased. . . . "What's a hundred thousand if we can prevent the world from being destroyed?" seems to be the image impressed upon these unlearned minds. We wept when the country of India had announced its first atomic bomb . . . we knew that it was possible, but felt that the government would realize its spiritual position. The exploding of an atomic bomb upon thousands will not be done by the West—this deed will be accomplished by an Eastern country, wiping out thousands of years of karmic progress in one quick, non-thought-out action of hatred and revenge.

We had told the medium in prior trance that Golda Meier would not be in office sometime in the 1970's, that she would be removed. We indeed made the conditions around her most difficult so that she would be removed. Her choices were not selfish, not for herself at least, but for her country —and even though she might incur much karmic damage, she continued to make wrong choices, which fed those incorrect decisions that the Arab countries have of recent been making themselves. We work with those we can contact to prevent this atomic explosion, but the choice seems to be already made in the minds of several persons. We will continue to work . . . and those of you on the earth plane can also work to prevent this by sending light to all the heads of states in the world; by meditating on peace and understanding. If it is true that divine metaphysics can halt, arrest, or even cure a disease [*which it can*], then it stands to reason that millions of minds concentrating on any particular aspect of expressed love could indeed prevent such a disaster. . . . But how many persons that read this would be serious enough to give of their time to do this? It is said that faith has moved

mountains . . . let us see if it can remove a rather
large mound . . . [*Three-minute pause*]

Being a scientist, I am most interested in the recent experiments that your earth-plane scientists
have been doing in regard to the creation of the
human cell, the DNA experiments to be exact.
When they do create human bodies, life itself,
where do they think that they will get the souls
from? There will be robots doing the work for you
. . . soulless beings of a zombie-type nature, that
will be replenished of damaged cells by graft, that
will not wear out because new plastic parts of the
body, inside as well as out, will be available. . . .
instead of this investigation into something that will
bring more chaos and confusion upon the earth
plane, how much better it would have been had
these scientists chosen to discover the cure for
many earth-plane illnesses. . . .

The prophetic aspect of this trance may seem
negative, but remember that choices can prevent or
change the prophecy. There is very little time for
you on the earth plane to "get it all together," as
you use in your terminology. After the bomb has
been dropped, there will be much bloodshed on
the earth. The bigger nations will take sides in this
outburst and they in turn will oppose each other.
The destruction is vast—no country will be left un-
touched. The Middle East will erupt into a major
war, the Arabs and the Jews will not be satisfied until they have destroyed each other . . . and the
prophecy seems that they will. During this time,
your own country will be going through many
changes. The 1980's will see the last of your presi-
dents in term of office . . . the responsibility will be
taken from the president and given to several men;
at least five will be in the position that one man is
in today . . . this allocation of duty will work far
better than placing all the responsibilities and thus
draining all the energies of one man. . . .

Date: June 25, 1974
Time: 3:30 P.M.
Place: New York

Good afternoon . . . [*Pause*]

I am most delighted that our instrument has chosen to let us enter through him after a very short period of time. . . . . we are grateful.

The spirit entities who have been sent to prophesy the forthcoming millennium have been working through earth-plane mediums for many centuries, since even before the time of Nostradamus. It was, however, Nostradamus who first allowed himself to be utilized in regards to the prophetic warnings being given to those souls who are on the earth plane. The prophetic changes that were brought into Nostradamus's awareness—and he did not receive this information by astrological calculation—were meant to be a necessary guidline for the souls who were reaching out to a higher level of experience.

Down through the centuries we have worked through many others—in your own country, Edgar Cayce, Arthur Ford, Eileen Garrett, Jane Roberts, and the medium we are utilizing at this moment. We chose these because they had each been spiritually and psychically progressed in past incarnations. And, although it has been difficult for these souls to completely understand their abilities and to always utilize them in the manner which would best serve their fellow soul travelers—and thus themselves—they have accomplished much. Unfortunately, excepting for a minority, earth-plane souls avoid the teachings and words of those from our side of experience and strive ever more rapidly towards an increasing materialism and its ill effects.

If you carefully scan the prophecies of these mediums, you will see a similarity and an alikeness in those predictions which affect many of the world's conditions and future situations. There are those prophets who are able to see not only the chance situations, but the choices that people will make under certain conditions. This discernment of choice is what makes some prophets seemingly have a higher degree of accuracy in their prophecies.

Nostradamus gave the earth plane countless prophecies which have endured the longest period of time and have held the most interest for the souls who have inhabited the earth plane over the ages. This was despite Nostradamus himself, for he set out to carefully veil the meaning of the prophecies as they were given to him in altered states of consciousness. It was his own idea to mask the prophecies by including them in poetic quatrains. He did this because, first, he did not have complete faith in the prophecies as given to him. Also, he thought that by camouflaging them they would live and be interpreted as having different meanings at various times in history, thus always being relevant and alive. He desired to keep his name going throughout recorded time. Nostradamus got caught up in an ego trip that he since has had to make right in many successive incarnations.

When the veil is stripped away from Nostradamus's prophecies, and especially when viewed after they have occurred, realization that there can be but one way to correctly interpret them is very much evident. Nostradamus was also fearful of the things he foresaw; whether they were true or not, he felt that there could be mass panic if the majority of peoples had access to the prophecies and their correct meanings. His prophecies, now more than ever, should be heeded, for they are true and can be confirmed.

Nostradamus' prophesy stated that in the area opposite what was Babylon, there would occur a great outpouring of blood that would make the land, sea, and air seem tainted. He went on to state that quarreling, hunger, plague, and confusion would then rule. Nostradamus was referring to the countries in the Near and Middle East, which are opposite that which was Babylon—this particular quatrain refers to the time period of today and the taintedness he spoke of are the effects of the atomic bombs or nuclear weapons which will be utilized there during the next twenty-five years.

This will be the beginning of the end of life as it is known on the earth plane. There will be no hiding from this destruction, which will strike even the remote sections of America. Atomic dust will be carried over the earth's fields, mountains, and streams. The oceans will yield up dead sea life; there will be a time when the oceans will have no living things in them and will have to be replenished by man from certain places where various sea life are now kept. [This must mean aquariums, zoos, etc.]

Nostradamus made constant reference to the year just prior to the commencement of the twenty-first century as the one in which most of the destruction and change would take place. This should be interpreted as meaning not only the year 1999 but the years preceding it—in fact, from now [1974] until the first years of the twenty-first century.

At the start of the new century, most of the changes will have taken place and the millennium will have begun; the thousand years of peace and spiritual enlightenment will then proceed.

In retrospect, the years onward from the birth of Jesus will be looked on as being the most bloody and violent in man's experience on the earth plane. It has been because of the misinterpretation of the words and messages of this most holy teacher who had been brought into the earth's vibrations to move men towards truth, love, and brotherhood. If the selfish bondage-holding hierarchy of the Churches would but release *all* the words and teachings of Jesus, there would be no way of misinterpretation of the knowledge which was imparted to this great teacher and medium by the higher forces of the spiritual realms.

Fear. . . . [*Long pause*]

It has been fear and greed which has held back this knowledge from those who have been in such need of it over the centuries. Jesus' psychic nature, his healing aspects, and his ability to look into the past, present, and future of one's soul has been carefully eliminated from that which you know of his life by those in the Church who wished to withhold the information in order that they themselves might better keep their people in bondage. It will not be before too long that many other books of the New Testament—as you refer to it—will be made available to the earth-plane peoples.

The Vatican holds the keys to these so-called lost books, as it had done with the Apocrypha. After the time of between nine and thirteen years [*which would be from 1983 to 1987, dating from this session*] the Pope on the Papal throne at that time will demand that the complete enlightened knowledge and teachings of Jesus be passed onto the peoples of the earth. The karma of so many Popes who kept secret that which they truly knew of Jesus is heavy upon their heads. They could have brought peace and love into the world, but they could not bear to do this at the expense of the organized Church. . . . [*Long pause*]

The time is now . . . the millennium is at hand. Gather yourselves together in groups that can withstand the physical, mental, and spiritual turmoil that has only begun to take place. Build your inner awareness and spiritual strength, for you will need all you can to withstand the changes, the conflicts, and the confusion. That which we have brought through this medium in the past is now happening and will continue—at least until those on the earth-plane level of experience commence to make correct choices. . . . [*Short pause*]

I see that there are those of you who will ask, "And what are the right choices?" There isn't one of you who does not know the right choice in any given situation; the true, rightful answer is always within. But, reaching within oneself remains the problem for so many of you who are caught up in the material and cannot even begin to fathom the idea of going inward. You rationalize the correct choices out of your minds to coincide with some materialistic viewpoint or gain.

The thieves who are in high governmental positions today *can* be replaced by those with higher spiritual standards . . . but then, would that not affect how you in turn will act and make decisions? The unconscious rationalization is that if those who are in high elected offices can get away with the deceit, the cheating, the murder—if they can do these things—then why can't the rest of you do likewise? It is a shoddy rationalization at best . . . and a devastating karmic situation at worst. . . .
[*Long pause*]

The physical changes of geography will commence from the year 1979 onward . . . tides will rise sharply as the ice begins to flow once again as it did thousands of years ago. . . .Why else do your countries send men and spend millions to investigate the Antarctic and the two poles? It is to check the melting of the Ice, which they already know of; it is to see how much water might overflow the land areas . . . and as each nuclear weapon is exploded, the earth shifts a little more, causing the vast Ice areas to shift, heat, and melt. . . .

From the rising of the oceans, and the earthquakes, and the reappearance of great land masses [*Atlantis*] your physical world will indeed change . . . but will this be warning enough? Will not your clever scientists say that it is merely a physical change, a natural occurrence, one that holds no spiritual significance? Years ago, these same scientists believed that all forms of sickness were of a physical nature, a change in the body—now they have come to realize that most illness is of a psychosomatic nature.

What will your scientists say when Japan begins to sink into the sea? When the West Coast of America is split into at least four quarters? When the East Coast of America is inundated by tons of ocean water? When the great land area that separated America from Europe once again rises out of the ocean?

Punishment? Is that what you ask? No, it is in no form a punishment. It will be the choice of earth-plane souls which will bring about these catastrophes. It is the unconscious telekinesis of the majority of those who are steeped in negation. There have been countless earthquakes and tidal waves of enormous gravity in the East, yet these countries have survived. Most notably the country of Japan would have been destroyed if it had not been for the spiritual awareness of the vast numbers of Japanese who, through meditation and natural telekinesis, held off the negative conditions of the sky, ocean, and land changes . . . but now, as the Japanese shed their spirituality, they lose this natural protection, this faith in the higher forces which has been with them throughout their history. As they sought material gain at the expense of other peoples and themselves, the negative weather and geological changes could no longer be held from their land. The Japanese way of meditating on the positive aspects of life, on earth and for future incarnations, is fast disappearing. . . . [*Long pause*]

America . . . once the hope of the earth plane . . . the souls who came to America in desperation seeking a place where they might express freedom of choice and have peace . . . how quickly this spirituality began to abate. . . . When the first black man was sold into slavery on America's shores, when the first red man was murdered in the name of Jesus or some European King, when these crimes against fellow human souls proceeded to take place, the spiritual, divine protection commenced to be held off by the very negative vibrations of those involved in the atrocities. . . .

The power to make the choices that would make America the spiritual refuge it was meant to be has been continually denied by the majority. . . . The highly evolved Abraham Lincoln, sent to the earth plane in a physical form to help break the bondage . . . the seance room often written about that was supposedly in the White House was no myth . . . it did indeed exist and it was Abraham Lincoln who contacted us directly, not his wife. It was Mary Lincoln who shouldered the blame of seeking a higher level of experience to protect her husband from those who would have attacked him for doing so . . . but it was Abraham Lincoln's awareness, received through meditations, which afforded him the ability to compose the brief but completely evolved speeches that were his. . . . The text of the Emancipation Proclamation was afforded Abraham Lincoln during a seance, the words carefully chosen to prevent an even greater outcry than did occur after the words were publicly spoken.

How suitable for all peoples in your own era are the words given to Lincoln from the higher realms of experience—his plea for an abstenance from all forms of violence unless necessary in self-defense, and that all shall be equal, could have been first spoken today.

Lincoln's Gettysburg Address was direct automatic writing. In a semi-trance state of consciousness Lincoln received the words which must be assimilated in all the peoples of the earth plane at this time. If I might quote this ever-progressed soul, who has been reincarnated at this time in your country and will be one who will again appear on the horizon of politics: quote,—"It is rather for us to be here dedicated to the great task remaining before us—that from these honored dead we take increased devotion to that cause for which they gave the last full measure of devotion—that this nation, under

God, shall have a new birth of freedom—and that government of the people, by the people, for the people, shall not perish from the earth."

Lincoln transcribed this most spiritual of messages and kept it in its entirety except for one change. The exact words given him were: *from these souls that have progressed onward, we take increased devotion.* Lincoln felt that the speech would have better acceptance if he changed this to: *from these honored dead.*

Throughout the history of your nation we have attempted to work through those in high positions. Even those who do accept our awareness at the outset of their careers usually turn away from it for some materialistic power. John F. Kennedy was the last of your higher elected persons whom we worked through, but he too became involved in a material, self-gain illusion.

There has been no contact with any of those in office—in your own country as well as in others—for over a decade. However, starting with the next election [*1976*] there will be those souls who have had spiritual enlightenment in previous lives and who will be seeking high political stations. It will be the choice of the people to ascertain this spirituality.

Do not be deceived as you have been in the past ten years. Do not decide who will be in office from what you see and hear on television. Television is a hypnotic device and has been utilized in such manner to manipulate thousands of minds into acting in a negative way. Meant for the purpose of knowledge through enlightenment, television has been used in negative ways to promote those who seek power on all levels of experience. What good television might be in regards to awareness teaching methods—and realize how it has failed by presenting only the base, lower aspects of human and spiritual advancement. . . . the Nixon debacle is not a chance, singular occurrence. . . . [*One-minute pause*]

Choices . . .

Though love, brotherhood, and understanding are now openly ridiculed by even your most intellectually advanced minds—though these aspects are frowned upon by the seemingly ever-hip and with-it multitudes—do not be taken in by its negation . . . remember, it is not too late to make the correct choice in any given situation.

The opportunities for the prophecies spoken in these trances are not only probable, they are almost firm, unchangeable. But they can be prevented, turned around. The negation can be thrown off even at this late stage. Time is of the essence. . . .

Time is the prophecies.

The prophecies are opportunities of time with but the outcome left to the choices of those on the earth plane . . . this outcome of the prophetic situations is yours to make, yours to choose.

And, if the choices the earth-plane souls make are positive, then the prophecy contained in one of Nostradamus's quatrains will not only see fruition, but will be everlasting.

Nostradamus said that the walls shall change from brick to marble and that peace shall reign for seven times fifty years. Joy to mankind will be proclaimed; the aqueducts shall be rebuilt and there will be health, abundance of fruits, joys, a time of song for those on the earth. All of this Nostradamus predicted would follow the war and destruction he foresaw in the earlier prophecies. And it will indeed be so, but I say that the time of destruction can be circumvented, can not only be delayed but changed into the millennium without the devastation. Choice. . . . [*short pause*]

The medium is quite depleted, we have overextended our stay. . . . I will depart this instrument and hope that I can bring words to you again. . . .

Remember . . . above all else—we do care. . . .

I came out of this trance feeling quite refreshed, despite Dr. Stanley's concern about depletion. I went downstairs to the kitchen and made a cup of herb tea. The tape was then rewound and played back. Again, I found many elements of the trance that were certainly not to my own way of thinking. I realized that Dr. Stanley's message was meant for myself in a very personal way as well as for everyone who might hear his words.

I put down the cup of tea. The tape had played out. I watched a heavy mist cover the rain-swept mountainside which I can see from my living room window. I sat motionless for several moments.

It was time for me to do some choosing of my own.

SEVEN

Epilogue

Mind being the next frontier, let us face it directly and honestly. Every aspect of the mind must be investigated, especially the subconscious. We must tear ourselves away from the tricksters, the mentalists and, just as importantly, those scientists who approach ESP and prophecies as if these intangibles did not exist, instead of with a positive approach.

In the late 1960's and early 1970's I was a frequent guest on countless TV and radio programs. One such New York City–based radio show was hosted by Barry Gray (WMCA), a man whose complete disbelief in things of a parapsychological nature did not deter him from having occasional guests on his program who were in some way connected with the paranormal aspects of the mind.

I believe that I was asked back on the program several times because of events that Mr. Gray could not materially explain, other than to admit that they were indeed paranormal in some way. On one of my initial appearances with Barry Gray, I decided to commit some "psychic effects"—that would stick in his mind. At that time, radio and TV hosts had verbally taken me over the coals for my beliefs, and now I decided to offer them a bit of proof of my ability.

I was to appear on the show on Tuesday, October 3, 1967. Miss Lele Rolontz, then talent coordinator and producer of Mr. Gray's show, had asked me to be on the second segment of the program, from midnight until 1:00 A.M. The first half would be devoted to someone else. Days later, I received a distinct psychic flash that the first guest would not appear and that Miss Rolontz would call me before the show and ask me to be on the first segment.

On Monday, October 2, I went to the office of the *New York Times* and placed an ad. It consisted of a photograph of me along with the information that I would be on the Barry Gray Show on Tuesday evening from eleven until midnight. The deadline for placing a Tuesday ad was Monday at noon.

On Tuesday Miss Rolontz called me. Before she could get out the words, I told her that I knew why she had placed the call, that her first guest couldn't make it, and that she wanted me to change my schedule and appear on the earlier half of the program. Miss Rolontz was dumbfounded. When I referred her to *The New York Times* ad, she was even more perplexed. That indeed had been the reason for her phone call.

Mr. Gray always treated me much more kindly than he did others with psychic abilities. I do believe that the psychic scheme I had devised had reached him.

On a succeeding Barry Gray show, one of the other guests was Kreskin, a bright, very fast young magician. Kreskin made it quite clear at that time that he was not a follower of ESP and that his tricks were feats of magic and nothing more. His work, he stated, was that of a magician, not a psychic.

The amazing Kreskin truly amazed me when, a few years later, I discovered him claiming all sorts of connections with psi, ESP, telekinesis, and belief in many areas of psychic phenomena. At least that is the impression he leaves in his performance in night clubs, lecture halls, and TV shows. At the end of each of his own TV programs, a popular series in the early 1970's, Kreskin always ended with some chosen quotes from renowned psychics, parapsychologists, or occultists.

Kreskin is truly a fantastic mentalist, but I can't help wondering, as does the Reverend William Raucher (well-known psychic researcher and author of a soon to be published book *A Priest Explains the Psychic World*), why Kreskin does not put his very credible talents in their proper place. He carefully avoids explaining to his audience whether or not there has been any previous planning on his part to obtain the countless license numbers, ten-dollar bill digits, and safety vault combinations. Kreskin confuses his audience with statements such as, "Perhaps some of what I do fits into the category of so-called 'psychic' under certain conditions. But, I think that my particular forms of mental communications as adapted for the stage are probably hypersensitive or hypernormal rather than extrasensive. In the manner of a concert pianist who has spent much of his life at the keyboard, the communication, a very earthly one so far as I'm concerned, has been developed through years of painstaking practice."

I, for one, am beginning to resent the professional mentalists and magicians who are always out there ready to cash in on the difficult, sometimes heartbreaking progress made by persons who seriously lend themselves to the investigation of psi and other related psychical phenomena.

Is there anyone in this day and age who is gullible

enough to believe that a person with seeming psychic talents can extract the headline of a particular day, after supposedly having written down this headline, folded it and sealed it into a bottle weeks before? One so-called "psychic" has been doing this trick on TV for years. Doesn't it dawn on those watching the program that the folded paper is not placed in the bottle at the time of sealing? Could not the folded paper with the headlines written just prior to the show be brought onstage in the creases of the "psychic's" palms, and as the bottle is broken by him, isn't it probable that the piece of paper is dropped at the same time, making it appear to have been inside the bottle?

Even if these psychic tricks are possible, is it not a waste of time and effort? I have just watched a highly touted TV show that had three psychically oriented persons as the guests. In their allotted time these two gentlemen, a scientist and an astronaut, and one lady, Evelyn Monahan, did more for psychic phenomena than all the magicians and mentalists have over the centuries. There were no "tricks." The scientist told of his investigations and how advanced data are now becoming. The astronaut related his experience with psi. Evelyn Monahan did some quite successful psychometry (out of maybe ten feelings that she sensed from the host's watch, he admitted all but two were right on the button). Most consoling and amazing about this program was that the host, Tom Snyder, quietly accepted the lady's talents. He didn't react in utter amazement or start yelling, "It's impossible." It was a big step forward for the media, ESP, and related psychic abilities.

Uri Geller, the handsome Israeli ex-night club magician, has made a fantastic name for himself in psychic circles in a short span of time. I can only trust and pray that he is legitimate, for if any deceptive practices are uncovered, Mr. Geller could set back extrasensory perception several decades, so accepted has he become.

He has put himself out on the well-known limb, and there are those skeptics who are dying to cut him down.

I shuddered with both fear and embarrassment as Uri Geller failed in his performance on the Johnny Carson *Tonight Show.* I have been Mr. Carson's victim myself, so I know what it's like. Airtight conditions on this show had been "instigated" by James Randi, a well-known magician who "duplicates many of Uri Geller's achievements with a combination of sleight of hand, misdirected attention and patented paraphernalia, and then calls them feats of clay."* This is not to say that Uri Geller indeed does not possess ability in telekinesis, levitation, ESP, and the like; my own belief is that he does. But to even attempt to work under these conditions puts him in the area of doubt.

As a magician friend told me, when a psychic places several liquid-filled beakers in front of him and selects one at a time, choosing those that have water in them and leaving the one with acid in it until the last, why doesn't the audience realize that the acid-filled one can easily be perfumed or marked in some way?

And more importantly, who the hell cares about water beakers, ten-dollar bill digits, and the like? If these people can truly achieve those phenomena, then they ought to put their abilities to use in assisting their fellow man in some way. Bending spoons with thought power looks great, but what does it mean other than when such a guest comes to dinner you shouldn't use your best silverware? Far better to use this ability in ways that will benefit others and the world. I wouldn't want Uri Geller to bend my front door key, unless it was already out of shape and had to be bent back, but I would allow him to give me psychic insight into my mental, physical, or spiritual awareness.

In my autobiography, I exposed many of the methods

* *Time Magazine,* March 4, 1974.

of psychic tricks, mediumistic fakes, and the like. At that time I also made a plea for persons who have psychic abilities to use them for those they might come into contact with—whether it be psychic healing, prophesying for themselves and those around them, or utilizing other paranormal gifts in positive or constructive ways.

Years have passed and I still make this plea.

Appendix

On February 12, 1974, I gave a lecture for The Spiritual Frontiers Fellowship, Rochester, New York. Several prophecies were included in that talk.

"I do not see President Nixon in the White House after August of this year," I told the large group that attended.

As I spoke the prophecy, an immediate outburst of applause rippled throughout the auditorium. This instant reaction took me off-guard, and I quickly added, "Just a minute. You don't know what the next guy is going to be like! He could be worse!"

Dr. Stanley had afforded me the above information in several trances. He had condemned Nixon on every count, even long before the man was elected to office. I had been on tour in November of 1968 when Nixon was elected and had to make a speech in Higbee's Department Store, in Cleveland. I told the persons attending this author-luncheon that the country would begin to decline because of Nixon's victory, that his administration would prove corrupt and that after his term of office, it would take many years for the country to get back on its feet.

"Nixon will not complete his term in office," I had stated from the beginning. Dr. Stanley had informed me that those on the spiritual level of awareness were working to remove Nixon in a positive way, and that he would not last as president.

"Whatever happens to Nixon physically," Dr. Stanley had said, "will be the result of his own guilt. He is robbing the people."

Even though I had a personal dislike of Nixon, I

161

thought this was a bit strong. But Dr. Stanley has proven to be right again.

Negative predictions for America seemed to be most prominent in Dr. Stanley's trance sessions. As far back as 1965 he told about the inflation and then depression we will have: "The country may or may not survive through the nineteen-seventies in an economic way. Financial disaster looms ahead for many in America, especially the smaller companies and individual businesses." Dr. Stanley's words haunt me every time I pick up a newspaper.

"Until the political atmosphere is changed in America; until the presidency is not one man's responsibility, the country will suffer. New political methods may be forced on America because of this," Dr. Stanley repeated more than once while I was in trance.

"The world will suffer as America suffers. The terrific economic burdens will spread throughout the earth. Not one country will be spared. There is hope that in the nineteen-eighties, as the earth souls turn more inward, become more spiritual, the climate will be able to change. Modification will be the keyword in the nineteen-eighties, and the people will not be leaning in the extreme directions of right or left."

Concerned about the seemingly prophetic novel 1984, Dr. Stanley was recently asked about the possibility of that book's frightening contents seeing fruition.

"Had it not been for the Watergate scandal and all that came out of it, your country would have been thrown into an atmosphere similar to the one described in 1984. George Orwell was, to say the least, a most intuitive man. He foresaw the atmosphere of the future and put it down in writing. No one in your country's politics will wish to follow in Nixon's footsteps, and therefore a safeguard has been set into motion. In this case, fear will prevent those who wish to take advantage of higher offices from doing so. Had the Watergate incident not been exposed as it was, your country would have continued on a course that would have led to a military takeover. Had Nixon not been so mistrusted by even those close to him, he would have attempted a takeover of the country.

"The person elected to office in 1976 will begin a new trend in working with positive vibrations for America," Dr. Stanley has promised.

Although many of Dr. Stanley's prophecies have seemed of a negative nature, they have all related to changes that would eventually bring the world and its people into a better, more positive, spiritual vibration.

His prophecies for the nineteen-eighties are much better than those he gave me for both the nineteen-sixties and the nineteen-seventies. Advances in medicine, for example, will be so great as to practically eliminate cancer, kidney disease, and birth defects. The confrontation between earth plane inhabitants and beings from outer space will be a peaceful one and will occur within the next twenty years. These beings will present new forms of energy to the earth, just in time to prevent the energy crisis (which will continue in the world for at least fifteen years) from getting out of hand altogether. And as Dr. Stanley has often said, "By the year 2000, the spiritualization of the earth plane will be well on its way."

Bibliography

Brown, Florence V., *Nostradamus, The Truth About Tomorrow*, New York: Tower, 1970.

Cayce, Edgar, *The Edgar Cayce Dream Readings*. On File at The Association of Research and Enlightenment, Virginia Beach, Virginia. Readings #140–10 and 5754–1.

Fodor, Nandor, *Between Two Worlds*, New York: Parker Publishing, 1964.

Freud, Sigmund, *The Interpretation of Dreams*, Austria, 1900.

—— *Autobiographical Study*, Austria, 1925.

—— *Delusion and Dreams in Wilhelm Jensen's 'Gradiva,'* (Austria, 1907).

Garrett, Eileen, *My Life As a Search for the Meaning of Mediumship*, New York: Garrett Publications.

Journal of the American Medical Association, July 3, 1967. Article on ESP and the Village of Aberfan.

Lee, Sir Sidney, *A Life of Shakespeare*, London: 1891.

Miami News, "Psychic Predicted Bishop James Pike's Death."

Nebel, Long John and Teller, Sanford, *The Psychic World Around Us*, New York: Hawthorn Books, 1969.

Pike, Bishop James, *The Other Side*, New York: Doubleday, 1968.

Plutarch, *Parallel Lives*, trans. Sir Thomas North, 1579.

The Psychics, Time Magazine (March 4, 1974, pp. 65–72).

Prophet Predicted Pike's Death, Miami News: September 8, 1969.

Quennell, Peter and Johnson, Hamish, *Who's Who In Shakespeare*, New York: 1973.

165

Roberts, Jane, *The Seth Material*, Englewood Cliffs, N.J.: Prentice Hall, 1970.

———— *Seth Speaks*, Englewood Cliffs, N.J.: Prentice Hall, 1972.

Sechrist, Elsie, *Dreams, Your Magic Mirror*, New York: Cowles, 1968.

Shakespeare, William, *Julius Caesar, Hamlet, King John, Romeo and Juliet, Macbeth, Henry IV, The Tempest.*

Van Over, Raymond, *ESP and the Clairvoyants*, New York: Award Books, 1970.

Index